Finding Your Future

By William Autore

Finding Your Future
Autore Books

Autore Books
722 East Landis Ave
PO Box 1082
Vineland NJ 08360-9998

Autore Books First Edition

ISBN 151 461 8540

Printed in the United States of America

Distributed by Autore Books

Finding Your Future
William Autore

Table of Contents

FOREWORD

In the late summer of 2011 I wrote the majority of the text that is laid out before you. I began writing a week after returning from a trip with a loved one and some friends. This trip I am speaking of profoundly changed my life for the better and at the time helped me become even more spiritually in tune with my real Self and the "worlds" around me. I also came away from this trip patiently awaiting a reply to a request I made during my time there. One night while reading a book before bed, the response came; it was so clear, so effortless and pure, that there was no need to question where it was coming from. I was inspired, and as the energy shot through me and I became aware of my instructions, I jumped up with somewhat of a childlike joy and went eagerly in search of a pen and a notebook. I knew right away what was happening and I was so excited I had to tell my Self to focus and stay calm. For you see, I knew that this was the moment I was waiting for, and that whatever I was about to produce was going to be special. As I began writing, I did not have an end point or a direction. I had only a theme and a clearly defined goal. The goal was and still is simple: change the world. Yes, I plan on changing the world. I plan on accomplishing this by helping to show others how to recondition themselves or better yet, how to avoid certain conditioning all together. By avoiding certain forms of conditioning, people will have a better opportunity to find their real Self, and, while doing so, instantaneously change the course of the world. I plan on helping to remind you of your essence and potential. Basically, I am going to reintroduce you to you. The "you" I am speaking of is the real you, the you that you may be able to see but are not yet comfortable with displaying. I feel it is important that you know what my aim is right away. This allows you to start to gain an understanding of the direction this book will be going in. This writing exists for the purpose of ridding some of the negativity and backward thinking that currently occupies our Earth. The focus is on creating positive new energy in the form of proper thoughts, behavior, and patterns that will empower us all. This writing was designed with you in mind but will only reach its pinnacle when you start to apply the truth that lies within its pages. If the aim of the writing sounds cliché, typical, or simply a misguided fantasy, then at least credit me for informing you early in the text. By my doing so, you can cease following along and hopefully save your Self some precious time and energy. However, if you would like to find out why I believe this book can create a new and greater world, then please continue to read. If you your Self are interested in living in a world full of better thoughts and smarter decisions coming from more loving, positive people, then please, continue to read. For those who are still on the fence, please allow me to elaborate in the following pages, for maybe I will spark some hidden insight. Now, I spoke of not only having a goal but of also having a theme. As I began to write, I could see the word FUTURE flashing repeatedly in my mind's eye. I knew that was where I should place my attention. While I am fully aware that the present is the only true time frame to live in, the future will come one way or another. You cannot change the world in the past so focusing on the future seemed appropriate. In addition, seeing how I was being guided through this process by more than just my ambition, I trusted what I was experiencing. You see I had help in creating this material. Whether you believe this claim or not, the spiritual realization I discovered while completing this book was unlike any other before or after. The feelings I had that first night of writing will forever be with me and I can now only hope it returns, if just for a moment or two. While I am the author of the book, I am not the author of the plan. So when you see the word "we" that is my way of speaking for and celebrating whoever inspired and helped to guide this information here. Equally important is the overstanding I gained of the responsibility placed upon me in completing this writing and carrying out its message and purpose. I knew what this was to become as soon as I began to write it down. I knew its potential as well as the pros and cons awaiting me as its writer. After all, I asked for this. This was my moment. Knowing that, I gladly accepted the responsibility required of me and I took full ownership of my role. I prayed to be used to help the world. This book is the answer to that prayer.

While reflecting after the book was completed, I discovered I was being prepped for this writing for quite some time. While preparing, though unaware of how I would help you, I knew that I was supposed to do so. It was a simple transition actually; one day I was told I needed to help others. From that point on I stopped looking at life simply for my Self and started looking at it for you as well.

After hearing the call I began a new path. That path first led me to myself, then to you, and then to that moment of peace when I prayed to be used for the betterment of the world. Now please understand that I did not see your future in the way a psychic claims to see an event before it happens. The vision I developed came about through a group of observations I began collecting over a period of time. I saw you and what you have been thinking about. I observed what you have been watching and I heard what you have been listening to. I witnessed what you have been living and experiencing. I saw your interests and activities, your neighborhoods and towns. Finally, after all that analyzing and observing, I was able to see what is waiting for you in the future. I was able to see this through patterns and forms. These patterns and forms began repeating themselves to me and suddenly stood out and no longer looked natural. I was then able to see what lies ahead if the norm continues. I have to be honest with you; I did not like everything that awaited us. I saw many moments of confusion and lack of Self-control. These moments led to many days of sadness, stress, and pain. Such actions and reactions could not continue in the future as they were in the past. I understood why I was seeing what I was seeing, but I wanted something different, something better, and something more deserving for you. It is important to note that I was in no way judging you or holding you to any particular standard when I studied you. For the record, I have not always liked what I saw in my Self. I feel it is also important for you to understand that a lot of what I saw was not entirely your fault. The fault, rather, lies in the conditioning you have received and will continue to receive if nothing changes.

While reading along you must know that this writing comes from love and positivity. These words largely come from a place of compassion and a need to speak up and out about the state of the world. I am in no way against you, and I welcome the day when we can succeed in practicing the principles of this book together. In essence, which is eternal, I am right there with you, in the classroom so to speak. You are one of my classmates and I am still raising my hand just like many of you are and will be. This is not only for you to use and benefit from but for me to use and grow as well. In so many ways we are the same and hopefully we will be going through this experience together. I am in no way an expert in all of the teachings this book has to offer. At the same time I am far from unqualified to present this material, so hopefully if and when my credibility comes into question I will simply smile at my detractors. Some may feel that I should be an expert or "master" before attempting to tell others how to think and live. I could understand that idea, though society does this every day and many of you fail to question that fact. To any claims of my inexperience I will simply say I am a messenger with an urgent message to the people of the world. This message could not wait for me and my imperfections. This message could not wait for me to be perfectly polished and fully prepared to deliver it to you. This needed to get to its destination as soon as possible. You see, this information does not need me; the truth embedded in it is powerful enough that the messenger undoubtedly takes a back seat. Those of us here on Earth who deliver or have delivered truth do not own that truth. The truth was and always is to be shared. There were many before me and many among me by the time of this writing that have made major contributions to the well-being of man. There will undoubtedly be many more of you to come. To all those who are yet to arrive, remember you are a part of the whole. Keep this in mind and never allow the truth you find to corrupt you for selfish reasons.

This book will challenge the norm. It has to or change cannot take place. It will examine beliefs, ideals, and society's rules. It will test the conventional format most spiritual writers of my time use to deliver their messages. However, challenges build character, and good moral character is being requested in the future from any and all that plan on occupying even the smallest percentage of its existence.

For years I have been led to this moment. This that I speak of is in the form of a book and its purpose is to change the world. Throughout all my setbacks and struggles I knew such a moment would be a part of who I am. I have been exposed to knowledge that was sent my way for the purpose of helping others. I understood when this information began to be revealed to me that I was not to hold onto it strictly to help my Self, but rather I knew I was in front of these lessons so that one day I could put them in front of you. Therefore, let this book help you find your future and discover the true nature you live with and amongst. Allow the words you find before you to help you learn the real passion, purpose, and plan the heavens have for you. Allow your Self to change the world.

Learn your Self by discovering what is true to you in your mind and heart. This way when one attempts to betray you, the other will speak up and lead you back to where you should be

WHAT DO WE HAVE HERE?

"To lead people walk behind them"
Lao Tzu

W hat I have been taught and told, and what I now know to be true, is that we have a life full of choices and opportunity to create the existence that we would like to have. For some of you this might be hard to agree with or believe in. Please give me a chance to hopefully change your mind. That is, if changing a mind is ok to do? Now, I do not think we have to spend much time covering the fact that we have not always made the right choices in life. From my view it is quite evident that we have not always "gotten it right." Life does not always allow us to be perfect. There are many obstacles that get in our way. Some of these obstacles, which we will be covering shortly, are not natural to whom we truly are. Therefore, we must aim to gain control in order to overcome them and by doing so, separate the natural from the unnatural. So, if we have a life full of opportunity, what would happen if we all made the right decision more often than making the wrong one? What could a life, your life, and our lives amongst one another be, if filled with the right choices? What would we gain compared to what we are losing? What and who have we missed out on by making the wrong choices? The possibilities are endless. What I am proposing to you at this moment, is that I wish to see what your life could become if full of right choices. I can picture you and that life. I see you full of happiness and peace. I see you full of real success and true freedom. However, my eyes are only my eyes. You and your eyes are all that matter now. The title of this writing is finding your future, but the message inside it is that you can choose and create your future. Yes, you read right. If this message is a new form of thought, allow me to introduce you to the concept. I am here to inform you that you get a say in the matter. Some will struggle to see it but if they need evidence of this "idea" it is all around them. Proof that this "theory" works is in my experience creating this writing. Furthermore, this is not new information, and I am by no means reinventing the wheel here. I am, however, creating a new tire for that wheel. I say that to point out that yes, you can choose your future, but you are not the only one occupying the Earth, are you? Therefore, understand that your future is connected to my son's future as his is connected to someone else's. I say that to also point out that while there has been tons of information on how to improve one's Self, I feel there has not been enough information on how improving one's Self can and should better the lives of others.

When looking at the whole, the room for potential issues becomes greater. For example, what good is this new Self of mine if the planet is too run down from careless use of its resources? What benefit does this knowledge offer of a choice to control your life if you are too unhealthy mentally to embrace and apply its worth? Of what value is this opportunity you possess to think positively and realize a better life if you are physically unhealthy from consuming a poor food supply? From that it is possible you may soon become dependent on medicine to live. This medicine will leave you in a chemical cloud. Therefore, how can you be truly proper when you have to function in a fog? Consider how difficult it is for a mother to be positive when her son passes on at a young age from violence. Too many tragic events occur from risky behaviors before our youth ever get to realize their purpose and learn that they can actually create their future.

I want to reach any and all. Hence, I must find the right approach for any and all. The seemingly normal one-sided approach many amongst us have sold you is not fruitful in essence. The lack of additional far-reaching information is unrealistic in my eyes. My scope of course includes the whole. Not everyone will find and live their purpose. Therefore, we need more than the norm. We need something for those who will not believe just as much as we need something for those who will believe. We need something for those of you who will find the "believe it into existence" idea as a sham. We need something for those of you who are around someone who does not wish to lead but who is willing to follow. Know that for some people following is purposeful. Therefore, following should be celebrated equally to leading because the one does not exist without the other. For others, hearing that they can decide their future is not enough. They will need to hear why they are not on track to decide the outcome. They need to understand what is in their way. Yes, their thoughts and attitudes are in the way but what has created these thoughts and attitudes? Where do these thoughts and attitudes come from?

So now when thinking of our purpose, consider what role it plays in life if you are only here to benefit your Self. You must think of more than just your Self when finding your future. This means it is fine to make all the money you wish to make but accomplish it without depriving others of rights, opportunity, and most importantly their quality of life. You see, you may find this book in the "Self Help" section of your bookstore, but this is far more than just a "Self Help" book. This is an "Everybody Helps Everybody Else" book. The information may appear similar to another text or source you have heard about or read, but it is not anything of the kind. It is rather all of them and more.

As I stated, I am not reinventing the wheel, just the tire. The wheel is yes, you can choose your future. However, the tire is how to fit your choice into the grand scheme and benefit the life around you. So once again, yes you can choose your future, but why should your decision only benefit you? Realizing the power you have inside your Self is the way or the "how to" in finding your future. This power is not designed to be used to separate and destroy, but rather to unite and build. Therefore, your choice in how to use that power must align with its nature. The difference in the teaching before you now is that it forces you to ask your Self how can you use the power you possess for the betterment of the whole. How can you apply this knowledge of Self to help others gain the same knowledge or better themselves? How can you create a new way for all of us? The answers are all around you. Some of them have been provided within this writing. The more you give the more you shall receive. If you can adopt this belief and practice it, then you will find that life improves for you the more life improves for others. Allowing things to stay the same here on Earth is unacceptable. A restructuring of the whole is needed just as much as an individual restructuring is needed. If for any reason the idea of helping your fellow brother and sister sounds anything less than appropriate, then maybe this is where you should cease reading. Find another activity to fill your time with. For those of you still following along, great, please continue.

*Not everyone is going to understand where their purpose lies. Even less so if they are not exposed to the much needed info about what is going on around them. This attempt would be lame if there were not a section on health, the importance of women, the need to respect our resources, strengthening our youth, and so on. What I am attempting to get across is that a book full of techniques to better your Self is great. However, there are already enough of these types of books in circulation now, and now we need something more.

*Before the text moves on I would like to say that there are some who believe that a personal restructuring is all one can guarantee. If this is true what does that idea produce? Does it not produce an acceptance of the norms in society on some level? My neighborhood is terrible but my house is nice. Yes, but what happens when you step outside the house? Explain to me again why Martin Luther King was marching? Explain to me why Malcolm X was so motivated? Why did Buddha teach? And why was Jesus followed? Not because they believed in your guarantee. Was Tupac Shakur at his best while he was on Earth? He passed on at 25 years old and like most to all at that age, it is likely he did so with much personal growth left to achieve. However, while here did he spark the minds of countless people for the better? Yes! It can take years to conquer the Self, but we do not have that long as a people. Did these men and countless others keep their power to themselves and accept the norm or did they change the whole? This notion requesting my acceptance of a guarantee bores me *

HERE WE ARE NOW

I love when you bow in your mosque, kneel in your temple,
pray in your church. For you and I are the sons of
one religion and it is the spirit
Khalil Gibran

It has been told to me that your future can be beautiful. Free of wars and senseless killings. Free of mass poverty and sickness. Free of racism and stereotypes. Understand right now that such a future will not come easily but it could indeed come. The hard part is that developing a better future will be up to you. You have the ability to decide how it turns out. It is yours to create. You have a life full of choices, from what you think to what you say. A life full of decisions, from what you believe to what you learn, that is what you have been granted. What will the outcome of your choices be? What will you do with that power? There is a lot of information to cover and much to look at in a short period of time. You see, we do not have the luxury of procrastinating; your future is happening as you read this.

Some will automatically shoot down the theory that I am attempting to get across regarding you, your choice, and your future. Change threatens people at what they believe is their core. It challenges their beliefs, their ideas, and more. We as humans have grown tired and ignorant, and even worse, complacent. This lack of proper growth could be a possible reaction to our fear, doubt, and ever-looming false Ego. We have in essence become closed off. We have developed this error in part due to our perception. This hesitation to believe often causes us to miss the chance to learn, the chance to change. Hence, we miss the chance to grow. The more opportunities we lose, the harder it becomes for us to ever correct our path. At times all we have is the moment to capture inspiration. A simple moment of clarity to find a truth that can connect us to another one. Yet we pass up this blessing due to our conditioning. How many moments have you missed? If you are reading this writing, do not lose this moment. What I am attempting to help you with is the easiest and hardest change you will ever face. The change should be easy due to the true nature that resides in you, yet hard due to the conditioning you have been subjected to that goes against that nature and is often instilled at a young age. There is a good chance that you would rather travel the easy way by now, so the path to finding your future will require hard work. Herein lies the problem because chances are you have become comfortable. Finding your future will require you to be uncomfortable at times. It is highly likely you will need to change something about your Self and "give up" luxuries, habits, and preconceived thoughts. Not to mention, this necessity will challenge the perception you have of your Self and the life around you. Chances are, as previously stated, your perception of reality is off. This error is not entirely your fault but you still wind up paying fully for the "glitch." Now I say chances because I am careful to not automatically group you. However, the odds are in my favor. Perception simplified is how we receive what we see, hear, and feel. It is shaped by various factors. What you see and swear by being beautiful can be equally ugly to someone else.

By now, whether you are on the right path or not, you should be analyzing your Self, attempting to see if any of the information you have read so far applies to you or someone you closely know. You should be sizing up the challenge set forth in front of you right now. However hard it appears to change, it is honestly easy to accomplish because you already have everything you need to make it happen. You and I simply have to stay on ourselves and recondition our way of being. We have to find our way back to our essence by locating the correct truth and applying its glory. We should do this out of the love and respect we have for ourselves and for life.

I now want to explain why I feel so confident that most of you should be able to realize your potential. All of you have the opportunity to grasp this theory, concept, idea, or whatever title an educated person wants to give this. However, not all of you will be brave enough to find your way back to your essence again. Overcoming the false Self you have become accustomed to living with will be the bravest feat you ever attempt. Equally, no amount of money or trophy will define your individual success the way overcoming the false Self will. This explanation I owe you should also help you realize why I believe you can achieve the goal that is embedded in this writing. As always, that is if you really want to achieve success. You see, when you came here, you did so full of potential and full of power. Those qualities are quite evident in the growth we have made throughout our time here on Earth. Just look around at what we have been able to create up until this point in our existence. Even amongst all this confusion and chaos man has found a way to produce amazing advances and works. This power to create comes from a Source. This Source is most commonly known as "God." The Source goes by many different names and titles. Some even feel that the Source is the universe or nature. However, no one besides a total nonbelieiver would disagree that we get our power to be, from a "Source." This writing is a prime example of that power. My opinion, which seems needed to validate the credibility of the writing amongst some of you, believes our Source is a supreme energy force. I would also say that while my opinion may matter to some, if it differs from your opinion that is not good enough reason to ignore the remaining text in front of you. Man has been attempting to discover that truth without a doubt for some time, and like I have already stated, perception is error. If our ideas of the Source differ, this is fine, for we do not need to agree on everything. I am sure we will not always do so. Yet consider the difference between what you think and what you know. Regardless of your faith, the common belief is that we have all been created in the likeness or image of our Source. My personal reasoning comes from certain capabilities and natural functions like instinct and intuition that we are born with and display without logic. Some of us are so sensitive that we can even visualize events prior to them occurring; this ability has a home or it would not be shared amongst us.

I believe that our "Source" is a loving, peaceful, righteous, and infinite one. This divine energy is an all inspiring and all natural one. This is a Source that all is bound to no matter how great or minute - no matter how "good" or how "bad." I also believe that our Source's greatest gift to us is life and "its" love is the greatest trait we possess. What if love and an appreciation for life were the basis of our thoughts and actions towards ourselves and one another? If we could think and behave in that manner, imagine what life would be like. Though love could be looked at as a concept, explain how a baby takes to a parent so quickly. Could it be that the baby somehow can relate to the emotion coming from the parent? If you smile at a child, they usually smile back. If you act mean toward the child there is potential for the child to cry. If the child cries there is usually a lack of some sorts involved. Smiling, at least in children, can normally be traced to love. Feelings like love are in you because you were created in the likeness, the image, and the flow of your Source. Therefore, your Source must be within you. Think of the previous statement like this: if you can get certain characteristics from your mother and father, is it possible to get characteristics from your Source? If I get my looks and my mannerisms from my parents and family, is it impossible to think we could have traits and characteristics from God? If God is indeed the father of all fathers and mother of all mothers is this theory not possible? Let us say for argument's sake that we do get characteristics from God. Would God pass on hate, fear, or doubt to us? If so, then you are stating God hates, doubts, and lives in fear, for that is the only way this could be. This could go along with the notion that God, our Source, is anything more than a loving, forgiving, and accepting one. This could not be a patient God? Surely not a God who has allowed us time after time to figure him, her or it out? I personally do not agree with anyone who wants us to discriminate and hate one another because of color, creed, sexual preference, or class, especially if they do so because they believe "God" wants us to. It just occurred to me that maybe we have a God who is unhappy with our particular belief in God. Maybe we have a God who punishes out of spite. Quite possibly we have a fearful and jealous God. The description of our Source as fearful and jealous is an error and an extreme one to say the least. The thought honestly amuses me more than anything. How have fear and other negative qualities become associated with the provider of life? So our "father," the father of man, is similar to our father in the flesh on the matter of error and "sin?" Our father who art in Heaven barely makes good on his rent, beats his wife, and abandons his children? Our God smokes cigarettes and drinks liquor until he passes out every night? Certainly this is not a general statement about all fathers and it is absolutely not a fitting description for the father of man, but God might as well be a deadbeat if you want to go along with these other characteristics "he's" been given. These negative qualities like fear and jealousy may make sense to you because you have been told they do. These negative qualities have no choice but to find their way into our thinking and into our daily lives. They now serve as a reminder of sorts. They are sort of like a cloud that hangs over us on a sunny day at the beach. No matter how much fun we are having at the moment, we know eventually the rain is going to come down and chase us indoors. These alleged characteristics almost seem to serve as a way of controlling us. God would want this? Does your father want you as his child to suffer? Does your mother want you as her child to grow up in a world full of hate and distrust? The answers to these questions are more than likely no. However, the creator of life would feel otherwise? Why does man constantly make God, the creator, the most high, a low vibrating human? Why do we give God our characteristics? We develop characteristics from our parents. They do not develop ours, or at least they are not supposed to. So why, and more importantly, how, would God act like us when he, she, or it, is God? If man is anything like God it is the best in man, surely not the alternative. I am in no way attempting to offend anyone and their beliefs with the truth I now believe. However, offending some of you may be required.

Pumping children full of fear, anger, and hatred is abuse. If a child is raised in a chaotic environment, they become stunted. So the question is what kind of parent wants their child's growth to become stunted? I do not mean to further offend anyone but I am quite puzzled at times by how man makes "God" out to be. God hates homosexuals? God hates the Jews? God made the white race the supreme race? This and other similar claims are error. There is no way around this lack. The only way to remove your Self from the confusion is by being greater than it. "God" is above it; therefore you should head in that direction

LOVE

"At the risk of seeming ridiculous, let me say that the true revolutionary is
guided by a great feeling of love. It is impossible to think of a genuine
revolutionary lacking this quality."
Ernesto "Che" Guevara

I am sure to create a stir with the previous section's
questions and statements. However, one of the reasons this was
written was to hopefully show you the confusion we are capable of
creating. Confusion will slow your future in developing. Confusion
is the result of other concepts that man has created. Understanding is
the opposite of confusion. In developing one's self and one's future,
understanding is equated to love. You and your future will not be
able to properly thrive until you and others present in that future are
able to show a fair level of this. Understanding can very well be your
biggest challenge in developing the future you desire because it is the
opposite of what you have undoubtedly been exposed to before now.
We all must have a great deal of understanding for one another in
your future. We must be patient and allow everyone to become
adjusted to new thinking, new action, and new conditioning. This is
love. Just as we have to remain patient when met by those who resist
new thinking, new action, and new conditioning. This is also love.
New conditioning will only come through reconditioning, and this
will take a great deal of time and focus for some.

Love is what your future must be built off of. It is the missing
ingredient in the now and will be the most essential piece to your
future's puzzle. This entire book could be written about nothing more
than the need for love. When love is present in one's Self, nothing
can conquer you. Love for your Self, your true Self, will serve as
enough motivation to move your mind toward continuing to grow and
expanding your knowledge. Love for your Self will also require you
to develop the proper respect you truly deserve. Love for one another
regardless of differences would delete doubt, separation, and hatred.
Love is your Source's greatest shared power, and its potential is
endless. This understanding is the single most important
characteristic to gain along the way in developing your future. This
comes about by not always settling for what is right in front of you,

but by searching for more. This is because love demands more than the norm.

Whatever you do, say, or think, allow your Self to do it with love. Notice I did not say "try." The word "try" implies there is a chance you will not be able to achieve what you set out to accomplish. There is no trying when developing. Remember this view on the words try and allow, and be sure to know the difference. So once again, allow love to find its way into your hearts and minds. Allow it to represent you. Allow it to build up your future. You may have to yell at someone you care for in your future. If you do so out of love, then whoever is the target of your yelling will not only have a chance to see love in rare form, but will also have the opportunity to learn during the process. A proper lesson can still be achieved now, which means growth can develop. However, if love is not in the mix, then the conditioning that the yelling offers could send one in the wrong direction, fast or slow. This feat will not be easy due to the conditioning you have already come in contact with. However, the more you keep love in your mind and in your heart, the more you will act out of love. Seeing how love is your Source's greatest shared characteristic, then applying it should become second nature to you and others in your future; that is, granted you continue to work at developing your core. Becoming conditioned to love will require strong self-focus.

Another opportunity to show love is when you allow your Self to understand another person's reasoning before rushing to a conclusion. Not everyone moves at the same pace. We all come from different backgrounds and have different experiences influencing us. Therefore, focus on the positive rather than the negative when interacting with other individuals. They may simply need to travel a different route and are at a different point in their journey. This is no reason to write them off as less then. Even worse than rushing to conclusions is when we feel we have the authority to judge others. Judgment is not required of you. I have often been amazed at the way we have judged or formed opinions of another for their differences and perceived lack. Time and time again we fail to see just how little our opinion and our judgment matters. So much energy is wasted on what we think about someone else. Not a "someone" who is in "power" and can decide for us like a politician or a leader. Having an opinion of someone who agreed to represent you in some manner is easier to understand. Equally, having an opinion about someone in real need is also understandable. What is not understandable is when we spend energy speaking down on someone who appears to be at a disadvantage or in a struggle of sorts. So often we comment on those who appear to be less than us, at least in our minds, and we choose to discuss and judge them, not realizing that we are really commenting on ourselves as well. Since we are all connected, understand you weaken the whole when you weaken your Self. We have become so quick to put others beneath us. We are so quick to say what we would have done if we were in someone else's place, though it is highly likely we would not be able to carry their load. Who are you again? Surely not someone who would judge another, for you are a person like they are, are you not? Surely you are not one of those who has "it" all figured out? Surely you have been wrong or confused before, have you not? Therefore, your judgment is an error. Understanding your Self, what you come from, and where you are going should help slow this occurrence of judgment and wasted debate. Knowing how powerful and valuable you are should help you to remain positive even in the face of negativity. Eventually you will realize judgment is beneath your essence and not needed. Last time I checked, you age as I do, make mistakes as I have done and will do, so it would be wise to focus on your Self and your progression if you cannot be positive when focusing on mine.

Another example of understanding is when you consider another person's idea or suggestion. This understanding is committed when you pass on instantly dismissing their input as if you already know it will not work. This, of course, is only if the idea or suggestion is appropriate to the situation and/or the moment, and not clearly designed to distract or slow progress. You show understanding when you pass on partaking in anything that may be hurtful to you or someone else. It is clear that we, you and I that is, do not love ourselves enough at the moment. If we did we would not waste our energy on negativity. We would understand it is beneath us to fall into its trap. You will surely need to show understanding when dealing with your Self and the improvements you will be required to make in order to develop your future. Therefore, it is essential to show enough love to your Self to keep an open mind and learn from your "mistakes." While you are learning, you are growing.

Love shatters fear, doubt, judgment, ignorance and more. It chips away at poor conditioning while simultaneously establishing new and essential conditioning. Remember, understanding is love, and love has to be the key ingredient in your development. It is what will always decide the fate of each and every one of you in finding your future.

At this time you can close the book and place it aside if you can truthfully say you understand the importance of love and just how essential it is in finding your future. If you undoubtedly know how essential love is in developing all that is around you, then this is where we can part. While the remaining text is full of essential information, the section you have just completed reading is the most important piece to the writing. By allowing love to motivate you, you will surely find the way. You may bump your head once or twice on your journey but you will eventually reach your destination. For that is the power love possesses.

ALLOW ME TO EXPLAIN

"I know where I'm going and I know the truth, and I don't have to be what
you want me to be." "I am free to be what I want"
Muhammad Ali

This idea that you are somehow able to choose your
future may come as a surprise to many of you. For others it will serve
as a reminder of the ability you possess. Lastly, it may have sounded
completely absurd to some and they have quite possibly already
closed the book and moved on. The reason for the hesitation in
believing that the idea may be true could be due to the feeling of
helplessness that lies in many of us. Too often we rob ourselves of
what we have to offer the world. Possibly the hesitation is due to the
lack of control some people feel they have over their lives, which
once again robs the world of its potential. What other reason could
there be for your hesitation? Maybe it is due to my lack of status.
Maybe if I were a celebrity you would not hesitate to believe in me.
Could it be that you feel I am on an evil agenda? That thought would
not surprise me; we have seen numerous people attempt to lead or
"change" life here on Earth by claiming to know a "way," just to
eventually reveal their true colors over time. I believe they have been
called false prophets. You have probably read the introduction and
learned that I believe this writing is "special." If so, you have
discovered that I believe I have been sent on some type of mission.
This mission is to help enlighten the world. Maybe this sounds
farfetched to you and that is the reason for your hesitation. Maybe
your hesitation comes from your own closed-mindedness. I
personally feel that if you hesitated to believe in my claim that you
can choose the life you receive, regardless of your reasoning, it is due
to some sort of false conditioning. This false conditioning you have
been exposed to has now found its way into your thinking. Now, I do
not wish to offend anyone with my assumptions. For while they are
simply assumptions, I feel I have fair reason to assume, just as you
may feel you have fair reason to hesitate when learning of my beliefs
and motivation. Whatever your hesitation may be, allow me a chance
to show you how even hesitation can be caused by the conditioning
you have received.

I presently believe people either feel justified for living inappropriately, simply do not care, or they do not realize they are living in such a manner, and therefore are unaware of themselves. All three reactions are in error. All three reactions are a form of false conditioning. People live like this quite often, every minute and every second of their days here on Earth; therefore, it must be a condition. Take this how you will but this is a lack of control. For centuries people have been told what to think, what to believe and how to live. So it is easy to see and understand why so many of us have relinquished the idea of thinking for ourselves. So many of us have become conditioned to trust, without question, in what we are being told. Therefore, you have accepted a life in which you knowingly and unknowingly settle on the strength of another man's word or truth. Who is this man we ourselves have never met or seen? Who is this man or woman that we blindly put our trust in? We believe in certain concepts and realities that have become acceptable for us because they were acceptable for the ones before us. Now, some will argue that I am asking the reader to do just that; go off another man's truth and word, my truth, my word. Yes, to a large extent I am. This is largely due to my belief in where this information comes from. However, I am also going to encourage you to not take my word without first questioning my aim, my logic, and my motive for delivering this message to you. Follow up your questions with your own research and you should easily be able to see the truth that is rooted in this writing. If you hesitate after doing your research, then you have full right to ignore this message. Others will recognize right away that I am bringing forth the truth. Those of you who see that will take this information and run forward. Either reaction is fine by me.

One of the ideas I am going to ask you to believe in is the power each and every one of you has inside of you. This power you have will develop your future if used properly. While some are going to refuse the offer, this belief in "you" costs nothing. This message is universal and has been told time after time in various forms, from countless individuals, all in an attempt to get the truth across to you and show you the way back to your essence. This writing will hopefully remind you of that essence, or for some, teach you of its existence. It should also remind or teach you the importance of living your life based off of truth. Life is a precious gift, a precious time, and a precious experience, one that we should take full advantage of living and learning about. Consider this, if you are given a gift, you are usually happy, are you not? So why would you react to life any differently? Life is the biggest gift you can receive. You see, without life we would not even be able to create the idea of a gift. Every day you wake up is a present. Start simple if needed. You should feel good every day you wake up and realize you are living. This approach is not always easy but it is appropriate. Every day is another day to live and learn, another day to grow and achieve. Now, some of you might disagree, because maybe you have lost the desire to learn, achieve, and grow. Maybe you disagree due to your perception of reality. Even in doubt your perception is almost sure to be off, if only in the slightest direction. This lack you may possess is fully understandable considering what we have created here. Some of you wake up and see your gift and start your day off mad. Some of you wake up and see the gifts you have received such as a loving spouse and happy and healthy children and do not find joy there. You wake to them but are not thankful for them being there waiting for you and on you. I understand feeling good is not always easy. This understanding is one of the reasons for this writing. The plan is to help us get back to where you and I belong. You see, I personally struggle with the idea that we are supposed to go without, to struggle, live in pain, and to be "stressed out." Why are we unhappy in life when we have life? Pain, stress and sadness are all perceptions, and these are perceptions that man has created. Every day we give these perceptions our precious power and attention. By doing so, we constantly leave room for error. I want to be clear and state that I am fully aware of physical pain. However, the pain in your mind is normally just where you placed it, in your mind. Could you possibly feel stressed because you allowed your Self to feel that way? Could you be unhappy due to an expectation you created and allowed to affect you when it was not met? Do you not have a choice in how you look at this "problem" that constantly weighs on you? Is it possible you stopped growing, learning, and achieving because you were distracted from doing so? Is it possible your situation is due to wrongfully placing your attention and focus, your power, on the meaningless "things" this life now features? If you are a child when you find this writing then you have just begun to achieve, grow and learn. The youth are always key because they arrive with less conditioning. You and your peers are the ones who have the most potential to create. The question to the children is, do you want to realize that potential or do you want to rest? To those of you who are referred to as adults, now is the perfect time to allow a new way of thinking and living to find its way into your being. This is, of course, only if you think or feel a new way is needed. One of the issues that may be holding you back is that you do not feel that a new way is needed. Hence, you are in essence holding your Self back. This would not surprise me and is completely understandable, for many of us are shut off from the knowledge that we offer to us. Maybe you do have it all figured out or maybe you are who you are, due to the comfort you find in blaming your behavior on your upbringing or environment? "That's just how I am" is the common phrase, and that way of thinking must be challenged. I my Self once took comfort in blaming my lack on my childhood, my "deficit," and on circumstances of environments and situations. For some time it felt good to be without, to struggle and to have a story of misfortune. I was somehow special and blessed because I went through all that I went through and was still here. Wait, but who was I and where was here? Surely I am not who I set out to be. Surely not someone satisfied with continuing the cycle I was on. Was I going to be someone who *almost* became successful? Was I going to be one of those people I used to hear of when I was growing up? Reminiscing on past glory, but placing blame on everyone but myself for not being better off? Someone who was going to allow the past's circumstances to dictate their life moving forward? What I learned is I have always been special and blessed, but not due to my struggle. I am special and blessed for being able to have the courage to overcome my struggles and regain control of my life. I am special due to my likeness. I am blessed because of my belief in myself and the purpose laid in front of me. Where did focusing on the negative aspects of my shortcomings get me? Where did blaming others get me? Where did making excuses get me? They got me nowhere, unless you want to count when I was in discussion with a like-minded individual who was conditioned to blame others and just as eager to find a way to justify their inactions as I was. Sharing stories of pain without redirection towards a way out of that pain is a dead end conversation that should not be repeated consistently. Negativity loves company. The courage required to overcome the obstacles in front of you will not be easy to find. Yet once you display it the world opens up to you. Change will not happen without courage. Building and sustaining a future is a challenging journey that will require tons of adjustments. Therefore, why bring extra baggage with you? The key is to understand and accept where your bad habits and your shortcomings come from. Once you do so, then go about correcting them and turn those weaknesses into strengths. You growing up poor in a present world that requires money may become a weakness. The lack of money to afford clean food and water, proper healthcare and fit living conditions can create more weakness. However, that lack can become your motivation and determination to change your financial circumstances. These strengths will carry over into everything you do and quite possibly everything those around you do.

Many of you in the West have a choice and now just have to adjust and focus. Then we will see. Children yes, you will be products of your negative environments if you are not able to see through the smoke, confusion, and chaos. Accept this and embrace the challenge. This acceptance will offer you a mirror into your Self and the actions of your environment. If you are not able to figure out that you are in control of you, you will be quick to blame others. You will attempt to justify your behavior by refusing to accept that you had a role to play in the situation. It was not I who made you angry, it was you who made you angry. Who am I to throw you off center and vice versa? No one but you makes you angry. Adults, do not place blame anymore, because you no longer have to. Placing blame on your past as a full grown adult is beneath you now. This action will take up too much time and energy; not to mention it will make you appear weak because you will always have an excuse surrounding you. To those who may have come across this material towards the middle or latter part of your life, it is never too late to better your Self. You can still contribute, still achieve, still change the world, and I welcome you to start doing so as soon as possible. The question to the adults is the same as what was asked to the children: will you realize your potential or rest?

Allow me to stress in this writing how important it is that we should all live our life based off of truth. So naturally, finding the correct truth should be one of the goals of human beings. Simply settling for a truth you yourselves have never investigated is beneath you and an insult to your essence. When you settle, you accept. Make sure you understand what it is you are settling for. Some people will tell you they are in control, but in reality, if they do not feel like they have a choice in deciding the outcome of their future, then they are being controlled by something else other than what is natural.

What do you want your future to consist of? Does your future have to look like our past? What role will you play in shaping this future of yours? Do not focus so much on coming up with your answers at this time, just focus on the idea of being able to choose your future. Focus on change and learn of its power. Focus on what you can control. You all have a future no matter what age you are. Your next thought is a new now. The future is that simple, but it can be so much more than that if you would like it to be. You see, your future is not just the life you are living at the moment. Your future is not just that career move you are preparing to make. Your future is your life after this life as well. If you are brave enough to choose your future, then we have some "work" to do. You lead the way, and let this information serve as your flashlight

No matter what your age, you are a different person than you were five years ago. Imaging the changes you can make in the next five years......

F.E.A.R.

"The first duty of man is to conquer fear; he must get rid of it,
he cannot act until then."
Thomas Carlyle

If you allow negative concepts to cloud your thinking, your future will continue as our past has. Your ability to fully understand these manmade concepts and their dangerous potential is essential to the development of your future. The number one negative concept on the list to conquer is fear. A simple example of fear could be someone reading along saying, "This guy is crazy, I cannot decide my future." That statement is fear based and comes from the years of conditioning you have received. It is important that you recognize fear and who, where, and what it comes from. You will find fear in your Self, in your parents and your family. You will find it in your friends and in people you interact with day in and day out. You will see and hear it in your media and from your leaders. You will hear it spewed, recited, and preached from every corner of the Earth. Fear is everywhere and is the reason for war, racism, hate, and separation. Fear is even the reason behind concepts like procrastination, doubt, and greed. Fear spreads, and spreads faster than truth. It is in our thoughts in regards to us and our nature, our potential and our fellow woman and man. Since you fear strangers, you live life missing out on the best life has to offer. What is it you miss out on? Maybe a new friend, lover, or opportunity that is right around the corner. You can come face to face with chance and fail to capture the moment out of fear. Someone is always out to get you so therefore you fear others' motives before you even meet them. You fear accepting and giving help, therefore you will suffer instead of asking for a hand, or worse, watch someone else suffer instead of offering a hand. Someone will think you are weak if you ask for help, just as someone will take advantage of you if you offer to assist them. You fear skin color. You fear differences, though oddly enough, you fear similarities as well. Fear is even in your description of God. The worst example of fear may be when someone is afraid to speak up out of "fear" of being punished. What is more punishing than being afraid? What better way to be controlled than to be in fear? What better way to exercise control than by spreading and instilling fear? People have become afraid of everything imaginable. People are afraid to make money. The root of all evil is money, therefore some of you use fear as a reason to remain idle financially. Meanwhile, you and your family are eating terrible food. I have personally felt far more "evil" when poor and hungry than I do fed and secure. People are afraid to be themselves out of fear of what others may think. People are afraid to follow their dreams. While I agree the steps required to find your future may be scary ones, not climbing them should be viewed as far scarier. People are afraid to leave relationships out of fear of starting over with someone else. People are afraid of things they will never come in contact with. Sadly, people are afraid of progress and change. This last example of fear is why this writing will not be read or taken seriously by a lot of you. This fear of movement is why life has stood still or has not become what it could be for so many of those who occupy it with you. Fear feeds off of fear and creates a vicious cycle. You cannot allow it to overcome you in deciding your future. It is important that you recognize this and not fall into the trap which has defined our past for centuries. You will need to be fearless in your future. This will become easy over time if you commit to ridding your Self of the fear that quite possibly lives in you now. A good friend and teacher of mine would be quick to remind you that fear stands for False Education Appearing Real. The way you rid this falseness is through acquiring knowledge. You move past this fear through asking questions and analyzing the answers you receive. You conquer fear by the way of truth. Once you learn the truth there is no room for fear. It feels necessary to tell you at this point that you questioning, analyzing, and recognizing qualities in your parents, family, and friends will be essential in the development of your future. This is essential because this is where some of your most severe "fear" conditioning can come from. If nothing else, this is normally where your first dose of this conditioning comes from. The good news is fear can only control you if you allow it to, once again reminding you that you are in control of you. Search your Self for fear. A quick glance will likely produce little. Go deep inside your Self and be honest. This process will be difficult, but "stripping" your Self is a must for you and your future. Understand this idea and adopt it when needed.

DOUBT

"There is no better than adversity, every defeat, every heartbreak,
every loss, contains its own seed, its own lesson on how
to improve your performance next time"
Malcolm X

Many of you will unfortunately doubt your Self at
some time, either while reading this writing or at some point in the
near future. Many more of you will quickly recall a time when you
doubted your Self in the past. It is essential that you immediately
begin to recognize any hesitation in moving towards finding your
future. It is also essential to recognize any doubt that is alive in those
who you are consistently around. Once you identify their knack for
being indecisive, move far away from the trap that awaits you. Many
of your peers will contribute to this pitfall of suspicion by creating
the doubting thought in your mind to begin with. Others will foster
the doubt in you by failing to live up to the expectation you have of
them. "Systems" like schools, churches, and groups will construct
and house this confusion in you as well. Many adults have and
undoubtedly will inspire uncertainty in children. This finding is one
reason why it is essential for us to show love when nurturing and
correcting the youth. Doubt is so strong it will prevent you from
properly capturing a moment. We are over here experiencing the now
and you are off to the side wondering how you are perceived. We are
here enriching ourselves waving for you to join us, and you are off
somewhere due to a thought that you and you alone believe to be real.
Understand right now that someone will always have something
negative to say about what you wish to do and/or how to do what it
is you are already doing. If you allow someone else's opinion to
create doubt in you and your ability to achieve or complete your
"task," then you are displaying an error. So what if they think you
cannot achieve what it is you want to achieve? If that is true, you will
eventually learn it on your own one way or another. Therefore, why
allow their opinion to penetrate your thinking?

Doubt can cause a man to kill. Doubt can cause a beautiful
young woman to feel unattractive. These thoughts are just that,
thoughts. If you give in, then your thoughts will develop into real

tangible situations and events. Doubt is only thought, nothing more than that. However, when you give that thought power by acting on it and allowing it to dictate your life, you will soon fall victim to a vicious cycle of questioning and second guessing. An example of acting on doubt would be if you start to feel differently about your Self after observing someone with a lot of wealth. You view this other person as a success. You see what they "have" and wonder how they became so successful while you struggle. You then compare your current "position" in life to their "position." Unless you have attained success, which is more than likely wealth equal to or greater than theirs, you may very well begin to doubt your Self. The place you have reached in life does not satisfy you now. Next, you begin thinking of all the reasons why you are not "better off." These reasons are more than likely stressful or negative. If you do this or have done this, understand that evaluating your "position" incorrectly will more than likely stir up past thoughts and feelings. These past thoughts and feelings will more than likely be viewed as "failures" and setbacks to you. This will produce more conditioning. This process is an error. This way of thinking is not necessary. While there is nothing wrong with looking at someone else's position in life and using that as motivation, the only person you need to compete with is you. The key is to believe. Believe in you, your ability, and your worth. Do not question or second guess your Self once you are aware of your greatness; do not fall victim to doubt. You will know when, even if you do not know how and why. The correct process looks like such. After perceiving another's success and looking at your "lack," honestly evaluate your Self. First, ask what success means to you. Next, ask what is in your way of attaining success. More than likely it is you who are in the way. Therefore, get out of your way and go create your version of success. While doing so, do not stop until you have satisfied the calling that is echoing within you.

Being aware of your negative thoughts and feelings is a step in the right direction to learning your Self. Being able to prevent them from becoming weak emotions and poor decisions is an even bigger step in the right direction to a successful tomorrow. Learning your Self and learning to be in control will help you develop a smart, loving, and honest future. Once you are in control, you then become able to give power to what you want and what is proper. Getting to know your Self, your real true Self, should be a welcomed experience for you while here on Earth. Use your time now to learn so you can represent your Self properly. So many of us are not displaying our real Self at the moment and this is one reason for the present conditions we face. Controlling your thoughts and feelings is essential because they will eventually become something you can see. If this wonder and emotion is negative and becomes real physical issues, what do you think happens next? More of the same, because you are now dealing with those new issues the past issues have created. More than likely your outlook on how to deal with them is still going to be poor. Be able to recognize when you are thinking, speaking, or acting negatively and look for a way to shift your energy back to being positive. Represent your Self in the proper light.

Understand what and who is around you and how strongly they influence you. Analyze them. Understand how you influence them as well. Analyze your Self. Understand how right minded people think, act, and live. Understand how people who are not right minded think, act, and live. Understand what both can offer you. Understand how both can impact you. Understand how they can shape your future

IT IS NOT ALWAYS WHAT IT IS

"Tradition becomes our security, and when the mind is secure it is in decay"
Jiddu Krishnamurti

Next, I would like to discuss the impact tradition and old thinking can have on your new future. Both sets of conditioning have created and continued the separation, fear, and lack our society is presently living with. These forms of conditioning often go hand in hand. Tradition cannot exist without a past and "old thinking" produces tons of present issues. Old thinking can be found in many of the present systems, groups, and organizations throughout our world. Not surprisingly, much of the old thinking that is displayed is fear based. Those who live in the past do not see how much of the now they miss. People who think in this manner recycle stale thoughts and actions. They then bring that poor taste with them into the future. You should easily be able to see that if this past energy is negative, it can cause tremendous damage to us now, which will undoubtedly impact us moving forward. Tradition in groups, while appropriate at times, often leaves room for corruption and is used as a way to maintain control. I am not against tradition; I am, however, leery of its trappings. When nothing has to change – people, places, or the way things are, it is easy to become complacent or comfortable. Tradition can allow one to remain at the top when the bottom is now the more appropriate place for them. Change is movement. Movement is essential. When there is a lack of movement, corruption will set in. Everything in life changes, for change is natural to all life, yet your system should remain the same for all eternity? I am not so much speaking of the tradition that may be alive in a parent or grandparent of yours; I am speaking of the tradition that possibly lives in an organization or system you are a part of. Many political systems are full of tradition. This finding should be alarming because most of these systems are supposedly dictated and predicated by the people. Tradition and old thinking can prompt a person or an entire nation to go along with an idea they know is not right. Why is this so? So you can see the corruption yet you will still follow along because that is the way "it" has always been. What errors do those actions cause? When do these mishaps ever truly get fixed? Understand we are creatures of habit and form. These two forms of conditioning have been the reason for some nations being underdeveloped in industry, welfare, and healthcare. Also, these forms of conditioning have been the reason why nations have fought wars and produced chaos. Tradition in particular has been the reason why life on some levels never changes for the better. Slavery was tradition. "Whites only" was tradition. Men holding women back from working was tradition. What feels like tradition now? How has joblessness become tradition? How has homelessness become tradition? How has poverty at the hands of underdevelopment and corruption become tradition? How has brutality at the hands of authoritarian figures become tradition? How have unequal human rights become tradition? Is it safe to say the definition of tradition is similar to that of the word norm? Once again I am not speaking about the tradition established in your homes and daily lives. However, on second thought, maybe I am. You know better than I would about the traditions and norms in your life. I welcome you to change any and all that need to be changed. It may be the norm to use racial and ethnic slurs in your home. It may be the norm to not get a job or not go to school. It may be the norm to underachieve. Looking deeper, how has dependence on others become tradition? How has losing your physical freedom to cages become tradition?

Change is essential to you finding your future. I encourage you to go about taking the necessary steps to do so. In finishing these points, I am not asking you to assume that tradition and old thinking do not offer solutions and truth. Rather, I am asking you to analyze and consider the motives behind the action. Tradition and old thinking is appropriate at times, but so is what is new and what is next. Always make decisions free of Ego, selfish thoughts, and falsehoods. You do this by basing your decisions off of right mindedness and what is most needed for right now.

Do not be afraid to change with the new when the new is required. There were enormous amounts of positive energy in the past and many lessons taught and still to be learned. The trick is finding out how to apply the old approach to the new world. So always keep an open mind to the new as the future develops. If you are not able to keep an open mind, you will quickly become out of touch with what is now. Without being able to keep in touch, you will quite possibly stunt the growth of your future.

OLD vs. AGE

"There is a fountain of youth: it is your mind, your talents, the creativity
you bring to your life and the lives of those you love. When you learn
to tap this source you will have truly defeated age"
Sophia Loren

Old people, or better said "older" people, should not be automatically associated with old thinking. While many older people will demonstrate old thinking, so will many young people. Older people can have both a positive and negative effect on your future. This impact will depend on their beliefs and the amounts and types of conditioning they possess. If you are wise, then older people in your future will be well respected and looked to for advice and wisdom. The days of society assuming older people are weak and a bother should be long over. Remember, older people have many years of experience and knowledge. They are often the leaders of tribes and villages in some areas of the world due to these positive qualities. Many of them went without for the world you and I now occupy. Many of them suffered a great deal of pain and loss for you and I to have some of the opportunities we now waste. Many older people fought and are still fighting for the same goals you will undoubtedly accomplish. These positive findings and more are why you should always honor those worthy of honoring and why you should always remain respectful. However, while there are many great older people, there are also those who are or were stuck in their ways. Rather than looking at the world for what it is and could be, these types of older people look at the world for what it once was. Understand that just as you have become conditioned, so have they before you. With a little investigation you can easily learn of the world they helped to create and the types of conditioning they were exposed to. Not to mention, many older people have grown tired and feel like they do not have a say in the world anymore. This can produce negativity. That thought then produces a way to become boxed in. Boxed in by a society that has been waiting for their chance to box them in and up. The same society the older person helped to create ends up turning their back on them and views them as powerless. The older person then believes in that powerless perception and worsens the conditioning and the society.

Equally sad, many older people will not have an open mind to you and your way of creating the future. Many were alive during time periods full of fear, hate, and separation. Imagine if you had been misinformed for seventy years and were consistently acting out and living off that misleading information? You would have probably caused a lot of damage by then. You too may very well be "stuck in your ways" by now. For as we get older the chances of settling in seem to increase. This is a sad but true statement that you must not allow to define you and others in your future. As you become "older" you must remain open to new methods of achieving outcomes. By remaining open you will discover new truths and developments. As you become older, you should value your experience and wisdom and not accept being pushed aside by the guidelines society will try to place on you. Lastly, you also need to prepare for "old" age and its physical and mental adjustments. In the western world, as people get older, they seem to struggle with society's pressures to "look" a certain way. This should be of little importance to you in your future. "Old" age is natural and is in accordance with nature. Hence, its presence is unavoidable and should be accepted. All you can do is take care of your Self as best as possible now and prepare for then. You prepare by being conscious of your health and health risks. The same approach should be taken toward "death." As hard as that idea may be to face, the approach is appropriate. "Death," as it has been named, should not be feared, because it too is a natural occurrence. All living things experience this "death." If you look at life around you, particularly in nature, it may provide you with some answers for this "loss" that we experience. The remaining answers will come from text, particularly text from the past. Is that last sentence not ironic enough to remind us both of the dusty jewels from yesteryear? Regardless of your belief, this "death" that is feared and perceived as an end, is just that much more of a reason why you should enjoy life now and at every opportunity that follows.

Without looking into the past, the future would be unrecognizable. Therefore, please understand the importance the past has offered. This offer does not only provide insight in historical terms but also on a personal level. Without analyzing our past we may repeat our mistakes in the future. My personal past has better prepared my present and will undoubtedly better my future. This opportunity to look back at myself and keep a record of my thoughts, actions, and reactions undoubtedly offered me insight. It allowed me to humble my Self when learning of my errors, just as it offered me confidence and strength when remembering what I came from and got through. I was then able to improve upon my mistakes while building upon experience when moving forward. Analyzing your personal past is essential to your personal future. So as you head forward, do not forget your past or our past; just remember to not allow it to keep you from creating the future you deserve.

RELIGION

Seeing how fear, old thinking, and tradition have been previously discussed, now is the perfect moment to address religion. If you have "chosen" a religion then it may be wise of you to ask questions that pertain to you and your beliefs. Your faith in religious terms, regardless of your denomination or beliefs, needs to be questioned. This questioning that you may be resisting right now is only for the betterment of you and your future. This questioning that will make some feel angered or scared is only needed due to the conditioning religion provides. When you add up some of religion's messages and the way those messages get delivered, people may very well walk into church full of love and purpose and walk out several hours later full of fear and doubt. Religion perpetuates fear due to old thinking and tradition that occupied the Earth many years ago. Still this energy finds its way into the hearts and minds of people every day. While religion does offer the masses a positive outlet and a positive opportunity to help and serve, it misses the mark far too often for it to go unquestioned. The simple fact that it separates us is puzzling. Looking deeper, considering the fact that some religions have killed, punished, and sacrificed us both mentally and physically in the name of God, it confuses me as to why one would want to align themselves with that particular stain. Of course, when learning of those actions you would be sure to remove your Self from that association, would you not? Problem is you will not learn facts like those from your church leader or your school textbooks. Therefore, you must go outside the square to find the truth. While someone may offer an argument in favor of their faith, I will always go back to these facts and even rest on them. Separation was not good for human rights. Separation was not good for our schools. Separation was not good for the workplace, for one's salary or for equal rights. Yet, separation is appropriate for the belief in God? Murder is not right for me and you but just if done in the name of God? Some will be quick to say that the past is the past and this behavior does not represent the now. This is true for the church but not the people – we have never stopped accepting what religion has given despite the horrid facts that we somehow continue to write off. So in essence we are choosing the good over the bad, a choice that does not seem like an appropriate one to have to make in relation to God

Your God wants you to hate, separate, and confuse? Your God condones murder in his name? If this does not make sense to you, does associating your Self with something that has its roots in chaos make sense to you? If you find one of these believers, attempt to discover what it is they exactly believe in. Take careful notes while researching and think about what you are hearing, reading, or being shown. Some will be right minded enough to be able to see through the smoke. Sadly, others will sound mad in the insane sense of the word. Religious beliefs are so strong in some people's minds that they become reason enough to argue over whose religion is right and whose is wrong. My God is better than your God. We are going to heaven and they are going to hell. These arguments which are sure to be going on somewhere as you read this, are sad and juvenile. If you choose to become a follower of a religious figure, you can still follow whatever or whoever they are without attaching anything more to your Self than the understanding and the message that they teach. Meaning you can love and believe in Jesus without being a member of a Christian church. Religion directs the lives of so many people and will continue to be a force well into your future. How you perceive the information religion presents will dictate your future even more than it has dictated our past. And one last point on religion if I may. Please understand there is a difference between religion and "God." Please know there are people on Earth who do not belong to an ideology or organized belief system and in their hearts and minds they know the Source like you may. This is included to hopefully show you how your perception is your perception, and not necessarily another's truth. Therefore, the authority that you feel you have to say who goes and who stays, is false. Man's mind will never have the true authority to decide the fate of their fellow man's soul.

Your Source is not human, therefore the abilities you possess are greater than what any human could claim to possess on their own. This is why I feel so strongly about your ability to decide your future, due to where and what you come from

WHAT IS "IT" UNTIL WE MAKE "IT" SOMETHING?

"God has entrusted me with myself."
Epictetus

Be aware of labels and titles. Labels and titles are another way of moving away from your real Self. Do not be so quick to label your Self or identify with someone else's label of you. Man has found a name for everyone and everything. Labels, as well as titles, tend to breed separation. This movement is reason to be leery of adopting extra associations. Be careful and really consider the name you are taking on. We have a tendency to often wear these labels and titles. We then manage to become them. Boss, parent, executive, entertainer - these are all temporary and can cloud your vision if you allow them to. Yes, even the title of parent. With all these layers on top of you, who are you now? Where did "you" go? You need these titles for what purpose again? Do you need them as a way to define your Self; a way to separate your Self? Simply because I wrote this book does not mean I have to call my Self an author or even a writer. Consider this, what was God called before someone decided to call him "God?"

Simply because you are told you are something does not mean you have to agree with the assessment. People all around you are identifying with their label or title right now instead of identifying with their essence. "I am this, I am that"; are you really? Is that all you do, is that all you are? Categories to separate and questions that divide often come with labels. I am not saying that all labels and titles are bad. Just as I am also not saying you should disagree simply to disagree. I am, however, saying to pick your label and title wisely and remember what you are beneath and above that title and/or label. For when you do pick, remember to find you, the real you, inside that choice. You may be called "whatever" but you do not have to allow "whatever" to call you. You define it; do not allow it to define you. Remember that attachment has the potential to become negative very quickly.

Who decides what I am to be but me and my Source? Another's word or system who never personally addressed me, never asking for my permission to be called "whatever," no thank you

TODODAY IS TODAY

"God sent me on Earth. He send me to do
something, and nobody can stop me.
If God want to stop me, then I stop. Man never can"
Bob Marley

Becoming proactive and not waiting for tomorrow to complete a task that can be completed today is also essential to you and your future. Why waste time? If you are an adult, imagine how much opportunity you have wasted during your life. Time wasted by not really doing anything productive. What have you been watching? What have you been pursuing? Is it productive and worth your precious time? Are you just here and there and never where you should be? So much time is wasted on meaningless conversation and leisure. How much time is wasted on poor habits and choices? What are you wasting time doing? Who is losing out on your time that may deserve some more attention? I personally have wasted significant time in my life, even with completing this writing. What damage have my choices caused? For I am like many of us; still a work in progress. However, if you believe in reaching a goal as I did, then why are you not working toward achieving your goal as often as possible? Why have you not recommitted your Self to your goals more often and pushed through and past your procrastination and bad habits? Why have you not had more talks with your Self about your desire to accomplish? Why not push your Self a little more when you begin to give in to distraction? How important is this goal to you? How important is your future to you? Parents, if your child is so important to you, then why waste time elsewhere not doing anything positive or meaningful to anyone but your Self? If you need an example of focus and desire to accomplish, study the great Albert Einstein and his journey to relativity. His desire to understand the universe bordered on obsession. That same obsessive focus he possessed developed one of the essential pieces of the order you and I now live with. Understand if you want to realize your future, then you must commit to building and developing it as often as possible.

This is not to say you should not have fun and experience life here on Earth without a carefree attitude and ample leisure time. Leisure time, joyous activities and occasions with or without friends are essential to maintain. Do not feel that your future is a task; remember this is something you want and you should enjoy creating your reality

THE FUTURE IS NOW

"Learn to forget"
Jim Morrison

Learning to live in the "now" is extremely essential for you and every single person in your future. This practice is also a way to shed fear, old thinking, labels, and more. Living in the now allows you the room to move on from "mistakes," past attempts, and perceived "failures." Living in the now will also offer you a chance to move on from past troubles. Why waste time dwelling on a past situation that is long over? Why waste time on a trouble that in no way can resurface and has no place in your life now? Trouble equals negativity, and negativity equals a setback in proper growth. Analyze your "mistake," "failure," or "trouble." Learn from it and make the necessary adjustments to prevent it from happening again. Then move forward with new insight. This move is not always easy to accomplish but you should only look back into the past to learn. If learning is not needed then the only other reason is to remember a happy moment. Also, know that you will not grow properly without going through a perceived "failure" or making a "mistake" here and there. For it is natural for us to do so. This finding should help you see that there is little need to dwell on past mistakes or failures when you are not the only one committing them. Do not take them so personal.

Living in the now, or the present, has been stressed since the beginning of time and is essential in developing your future. This message and gift the now brings with it affords you many opportunities to start new. This start is exactly what a lot of us need in our lives at the moment. This start looks like new concepts and new education. This start is new thoughts, new energy, and new purpose. This start is filled with new moments, new people, and it is all happening right now. Therefore, your future is broken down into every millisecond of the present you are living.

You see, the truth is, the "now" will one day be the past, and so your time to create it, your time to write it, so to speak, is right now.

Yes, even your future will become the past one day. The truth is you have a choice in deciding this. You have a choice in deciding what is what*

EGO

"Whenever I climb, I am followed by a dog called Ego"
Friedrich Nietzsche

At this point, while knowingly running the risk of confusing or overwhelming you, I would like to attempt to explain the Ego. This may very well be your first time hearing about this subject which is one reason it has been included in the writing. For more information on the Ego, read works written by Eckhart Tolle. His book, *New Earth* is a pure gift to the subject and became very influential to me during my awakening. Our Ego speaks for us, to us, and about us on a daily basis. We have already touched on concepts such as fear, old thinking, tradition, doubt, labels, and titles. You will find Ego in all of these concepts. You will find Ego in your personal thinking and feelings. You will find Ego in your decisions and reasoning. Ego is why you have smiled and cried, just as it is why you have fought both physically and verbally. The Ego is even why you have lied and told the truth. Have you ever taken credit for something you your Self did not do? Have you ever "gone along" with a story or conversation out of fear of looking like you did not know the answer? Even better, have you ever felt like helping someone else to satisfy your Self? Think about that last question for a minute and be honest. Maybe you have gotten mad because someone did not recognize you for whom you perceive your Self as, or because they did not recognize your position or status? If so, you were acting out of Ego. Have you ever argued your point knowing full well you were in the wrong? Have you ever felt the need to "brag?" Have you noticed the way you do not acknowledge others when they are speaking? Have you paid attention to others when they are speaking about their success or accomplishments yet you cannot wait to begin talking about what you did, or what you know, or even how you feel about their issue? Have you ever made a rude comment toward someone completely unprovoked? Have you ever made a rude comment toward someone when provoked? Do you have a tendency to take things personal? Do you ever notice your Self playing the recurring role of the victim? Has it ever felt like everybody is against you? Well this is all part of the Ego, and it is in your way. An image, a perception, or an alternative false self you have created for your real Self is the best way I can personally describe the Ego. This new and other self will grow and grow and become bigger and bigger. Now this new and other self will begin to represent you. If you do not recognize this and attempt to understand and control it, you will soon identify with this "other" you. The Ego can block the real you from being seen, even in your eyes. Your Ego is why you associate with certain organizations and people. Just as it is why you dress the way you dress at times. Your Ego is the reason why you stay when you should go, and why you go when you should stay. Soon enough the Ego will pile layers and layers on top of your essence.

I am also unsure why and where the Ego was created. I have heard it came from the separation from our Source. If you wish to research the previous statement and the topic of Ego, please do, I commend you. Just as I welcome you with open arms to awake to the wonder that understanding the Ego offers. It is at the root of some of the confusion, chaos, and destruction the past has offered, just as it will lie at the foot of the problems that await you in your future. Please know that the less false Ego you possess and the less false Ego the others around you possess, the better your future will become. Shedding this will take much time because overcoming it is a constant, continuous challenge. It will require daily work on your part. The Ego is alive because of you. Therefore, you must be the one to destroy and rebuild it. Now, you have had some help in creating this other you. We have already begun establishing the fact that you have been conditioned. However, soon you and you alone will feed your Ego with your thoughts and actions regardless of the conditioning. The conditioning you have received has contributed to strengthening and expanding it, but it did not create your Ego, you did. I often wonder if some of the "truths" we have been exposed to possibly come from the Ego instead of from our Source, which is where many claim the truth they speak comes from. Maybe it was man's Ego that made him speak of the way life is supposed to be? The reason I am including this in discussing Ego is because the Ego can be a very dangerous thing. This is why I encourage you to follow your heart and research the truth for your Self. Do not simply go along with another "man's" word. This is true for even this word. Your future will depend on your desire to live surrounded by real truth, and free of out of control Egos. Ego is to blame for killings, for pain and sadness, war, greed, and lies. The Ego is the reason for your procrastination, your excuses, and for your lack of focus and motivation. You know you should wake up and exercise but "you" seem to find a reason not to do so. So you, the real you, wants your health to slip and to lead you straight toward all types of surgeries, medications, and spells to rid you of a sickness you wanted to contract in the first place? This sounds like insanity. You would never purposely hurt your Self, right? The Ego has been here since the beginning of our time on the planet and may always be present. It is certainly not going anywhere anytime soon. Your hope is to rid your Self of your Ego as often and as soon as possible. When you begin doing this, you will also notice when others speak and act out of Ego. It will become easier to recognize, and hence less easy to get caught up in. This should help you demonstrate a higher understanding of how to use love to interact with one another. Also, you will be better able to guard your Self from harm and danger. Would you like to fill in the blank? Understanding the Ego is _____ for your future.

Stop blaming others without blaming your Self for your role! Do not relive the past unless it is a good memory, time, or event! Only relive "failures" or "mistakes" in order to grow from them and improve your Self! Your only goal at the moment is to understand how and why you do what you do. Adjust accordingly

REFLECTION
"Constant elevation leads to consistent evolution"

Remember, or learn this now; ask questions in moving forward towards your future. The most important person to ask these questions of is you. Am I right? Why did I do that? Why do I feel like this? Should I have said that? Do I have to accept this? Should I believe in something just because someone else says it is true? Asking these types of questions and more should provide a deeper level of insight. This will allow you to become surer of your decisions and beliefs. These questions will also help to shape your thinking. Quite often we have simply believed in another person's word and thought without question. Do not be so quick to do this in your future or you will fall victim to another man's truth or lie. Asking questions should allow you to better realize if what you are reading, hearing, and seeing is real. This strategy will allow you to find your own way. For your future must be built off of as much truth as possible.

EDUCATION

"He who learns but does not think is lost,
he who thinks but does not learn is in danger"
Confucius

Lack of education means you and your future will develop slower. Get your hands on as much information and education as possible. Research Confucius and his belief on the subject and I dare you to debate his findings as a negative approach to develop one's future. After you gather your materials, attempt to share them with anyone who expresses a desire to learn. Education will prepare the youth in your future to develop properly. This group is the key to keep your future moving forward. Strengthen your youth. This must be a top priority. You do this through education; knowledge is power. This understanding is essential. Sharpen their minds and bodies by teaching them principles you have learned. You do this by exposing them to the correct teachings. Not only reach them with reading and writing but, more importantly, reach them about the need to learn their Self. Once you become educated about your Self then all other forms of education and information become easier to process. I do not know about you, but I know I would personally feel more comfortable in a room full of Self enlightened people who struggle in math and language, than I would in a room full of "book smart" individuals who can recite theories and formulas but cannot notice the beauty that lives in and around them. Imagine if you prepare a child, even before birth, with the proper conditioning and tools for success. Take a minute to imagine if, since you were born, you were taught that you should not be afraid of someone simply because they think or look different from you. That by doing so, you can prevent conflict much easier. What if you were taught since childhood to never doubt your Self when attempting to accomplish a feat or a goal? Imagine if you were taught to love your Self and be open minded to reflection and change. What if you were taught how to achieve greatness? What could the future become when its youth are equipped with a healthy balance of school and Self education?

The type of information put forth in these pages should be instilled in your youth as soon as possible. This is the education we are lacking in the present. Explain to me why classes on getting to know your Self are not being taught. Why are classes about meditation and the body's chakras not being valued? Explain to me why classes about the Ego and the importance of exploring the origins of our thoughts are not being taught at an early age. Why is the entire history of man and the Earth we have occupied not taught to children? Is a class on morality not as important as one on technology? Your schools should soon offer alternative teachings to go along with the norm, teachings that you feel are important for the time you live in. These institutions should promote togetherness and expose truth to their students. This information should better them no matter the career path they choose to take. Far too often in the past, we have left essential information up to chance and so much of it is never found. Allow your future to find what it needs. Show the workers why the thinkers need them and show the thinkers why they need the workers. Do this on an equal and respected playing field. Introduce the dreamers to the doers and facilitate their respect for one another's abilities. Understand there are people who probably cannot read and write as well as you can. However, these people may be full of wisdom and knowledge about the Earth, the stars, and the spirit of themselves. For as smart as some of you think you are, you know nothing. That is, if you are wise and not a fool. Wise individuals know learning does not stop. There is always something else to discover and you will be wise to approach life with that perspective. Make your future highly educated, but cover all grounds. Do not leave information like this to chance. Make your future full of thoughtful decisions coming from intelligent and Self-loving people.

There are many ways to find your future. What has not been said enough is how practical and simple some of those ways are to travel. For example, a change in diet can lead to a healthier physique. This change may make you feel and look more desirable and attractive. You may then begin to feel better about your Self and more confident. Now you are becoming more assertive and open to approach and be approached by others. At the same time, that new diet is allowing your mind to be free from harmful toxins and chemicals. Soon enough this change will allow you to think more clearly and operate at a higher capacity. This "clarity" can lead to endless possibilities.

These steps have nothing to do with going to church or praying. This is not to slight church or prayer in any type of way because you can certainly find the strength to change your diet through prayer. What I am stating is I did not directly speak one word of the Bible or "new age" rhetoric in detailing a possible way to find a new path. However, what I did do is present a clear-cut way to better your Self and take steps toward finding your future. This is why we need more than the norm because there are many roads that lead to the same point. Some will argue there is only one way. This makes one believe rather than to choose. Choosing relates to knowledge, belief does not. We need something for everyone, from believer to nonbelieiver, in order to create a better world. This is in part why this has been written. This book offers balanced insight designed to assist you in your journey toward a better life no matter who, what, and where you think you come from*

HEALTH

Y ou will need to become far more health-conscious in your future to ensure the continued growth of not only you but the life around you. You will have to eat better than the generations that came before you. Obesity should be lessened in your future. The days of eating fast foods and sugary snacks that not only negatively affect your body, but also your mind, should no longer exist. You need to learn just how much the food you eat impacts your mind along with your body. A thorough understanding of food and what goes in and on that food is essential. You also need to understand how important an active lifestyle is to your being. Movement is essential. In order to ensure the people in your future live long, healthy, fruitful lives, striving for optimal health and wellness must be an extreme priority. Health and wellness is connected to every aspect of our lives. Therefore, it is connected to every aspect of our society. The quality of health you live with reflects back to you and everyone else, whether you or they can see it clearly or not. Less disease equals less surgery. Less surgery equals less medication and pain killers. Fewer pills equal fewer side effects, which slows the cycle just described. That same cycle runs parallel to others such as business and trade. In the present time there is far too much money spent on producing less than desirable results. Remember, your future should become as efficient as possible. It should be one that focuses on the prevention of disease rather than the present way of dealing with it, which is by "attempting" to cure the disease. You see, there is no money in prevention. So it is easy to understand why we presently use the method of cure, where there are unlimited amounts of money to be made from visits, pills, and surgery.

In your future I urge you to not give others a choice in finding the proper information regarding their health. Rather, make it readily available to them as early on in life as possible. Do so continuously and commonly. In your future I urge you to demand that every doctor, regardless of their specialty, be properly educated on nutrition and prevention. This urge also extends to every educator, policy maker, parent, or any of you who ascend to power. Health cannot be sacrificed for comfort. You can make a difference in the livelihood of others. Imagine how much loss you will prevent if the approach to health changes. If this will be done then a thorough study of people and their habits will be required. There are many factors that go into the health of individuals. The motivation for this will be apparent the next time you see a child lose a parent to alcohol. The motivation will become apparent the next time a grandparent dies from a heart attack due to a poor diet. Your Source did not give you life so that you could destroy it by eating fake food and ingesting chemicals. Man feels so superior to animals, yet we do not see animals die from disease. No, unless it is disease caused by man. We feel so smart and entitled, yet we consume food and drinks that chip away at that very same intelligence and status. In your future I urge you to place health as a top priority. Couple that action with placing people first and money second. Give rather than take. Always prevent before you ever have the need to cure.

Look out for triangles, recognize squares and analyze circles

THE EARTH AND HOW IT'S VALUED

"When we try to pick out anything by itself, we find it
hitched to everything else in the universe"
John Muir

Another wise decision moving toward your future would be to learn about agriculture and community farming. Farming is essential for the food supply you will need. Do not write it off as less desirable and associate it by attaching an ignorant thought to the idea. Farmers and farming have always been important to people and societies and should be no different in the future. Encourage the youth around you to possibly take up farming as a career or a community responsibility. Be supportive of your brothers and sisters from different ethnicities who farm. Recognize the impact farming has on your life. It would also be wise for you to learn how to grow your own food regardless of your status, background, or financial wealth. Growing your own supply is important because you will know exactly what is being put into the food you will be eating. This is also a great way to save and/or generate money. Bartering and conserving resources are also positive qualities of agriculture. Understand that proper use of the land and its resources are essential to you and those around you. That is, provided that you treat these invaluable gifts with respect. If so, then the land will always provide for you and the others in your future. This leads me to my next point.

Moving forward, it would also be wise for you to become far more connected to nature and to the Earth. A simple question is this: Where will your future be if you destroy its home? The Earth is a gift given to us from the creator or Source. This gift should be treated with love, gratitude, and respect. Treat the Earth with the same care that a mother normally gives to a child. Some of you need to be outdoors more and in nature; it is actually good for your type of being. The days of obsessive building which requires the tearing down of precious trees should cease to exist in the coming years. Every new building in your future, if your future will have buildings in it, should, at my request, be an eco-friendly building aimed to cut down on waste and supplies. Think before you use paper for meaningless words and scribble. Conserve water and understand it is essential for life's continuous growth. Please understand before you cut down any more trees for new developments that we need trees to breathe. Yes, this may surprise some, but the trees provide us with oxygen. We should all conserve light, energy, and gas. Become smarter about what you are doing to the environment. Also, remember that life is all around you and is there as a constant teacher for you and me. For some, you can and should be able to draw energy from nature. However, this will only take place if you allow your Self to tap into nature's essence. For those still unaware, you are nature. Every cell in your body, every breath you breathe, is all a part of nature and the universe. Energy is real and is running through you and around you while you read this. While some will attempt to deny the truth, we are science. At our core we are one with the sun. Therefore, remove the ignorance of human nature to think that we are the only living organisms on the planet that matter. Our Source created other living organisms aside from you. So who is to really say who the better living species is, particularly due to the fact that we cause more harm to the ecosystem and to the Earth's resources than any other species. Man has been very arrogant in the way it has treated nature, which just so happens to provide them with just about every single material being used in this modern society. Not only has nature afforded us physical materials time and time again, but it has also been an example, or role model so to speak, for this life and the next. Nature has allowed us opportunities to find out what life is. Nature has also shown us how life cycles. Please remove this "I don't care" attitude and understand that your deeds mean something and will impact us even more than your death will. Deeds can survive time. Proper respect, care and love are good deeds. So show appreciation for nature. Show appreciation for our Earth. For a good example of how to treat the Earth, recall how you treat a relative or friend during a moment of receiving a gift from them. You are usually happy, thankful, and loving. Well name a person, place or "thing" that has given you more gifts in both the physical and material sense than the Earth. For those of you who will answer "God has," I will assume you have not read this section thoroughly and are unfamiliar with my views on the subject.

THE GAME

"Man is not made for defeat"
Ernest Hemingway

There is going to be opposition to you, your ideas, your dreams, and your plans about the development of you and your future. Not everyone is going to want your future to become a reality, nor will they believe in the way you go about making it come true. There are people in my life who still do not agree with me telling you this information, but so be it. Expect people to not believe in you or agree with your vision, largely due to their fear, doubt or dishonest motivation. For some of you, a total overhaul of your job, lifestyle, friends, and associates will have to do. For others, even the way you interact with your family will have to change. Do not be surprised by this type of behavior from your family and be ready to overcome the obstacles they present. There is also going to be opposition from people you may have never expected to oppose you. Some "friends" may become "foes." Some teachers will not like becoming students. None of this should matter to us for we have a future to develop. Therefore, be prepared to carry out your mission regardless of who is opposing you.

Now understand that some of you will be your own opposition. Yes, you will be your own "enemy" and your worst one. For one, you will question your Self when you awake. You will feel different and view the world differently as well. Therefore, an adjustment period will undoubtedly come. Remember, the "old" way of thinking had become normal to you. Therefore, it will be fairly easy to slip back into the norms you have known. Understand this and recognize if and when you begin to go backwards. It will not be an easy task to remove old habits and you may feel as if you are wasting your time with this "new" way of thinking and being. I assure you, you are not. Understand this may happen and recognize if and when you start to oppose your Self. You will also have to give up certain "likes" or interests while on your journey. Once again family, friendships, relationships, jobs, roles, careers, and routines can all take a back seat to the goal of developing your Self. You see, once you begin your journey and are practicing the skills you will need for your future to become real, you will be required to make changes to not only your Self, but to your schedule. You will be required to make more time to practice and focus on your plans for your future. You will be required to prioritize. This "new way" will become habitual if you are truly preparing your future and carrying out your duties. Soon this way will become your norm and you will see your new thoughts, words, and actions come alive. Rest easy, for those "things" you gave up will feel different to you. Those "things" you gave up will become less important and correctly prioritized. You will begin to look at life differently. You will begin to live life differently. You will begin walking on the new path that is being paved. You will understand soon.

Life is a mystery; the people you swore wouldn't, do, and the people you never thought would, will

AS ABOVE SO IS BELOW

"A physician without knowledge of astrology
has no right to call himself a physician"
Hippocrates

Iremind you to be open to different forms of enlightenment from different "sources" as well. Another way to learn about your Self is by investigating astrology. Some frown upon it for reasons unknown to me. Their opposition may be due to the belief that astrology is the work of an evil entity of some sort. This belief would be in error. Understand that truly getting to know your Self is an accomplishment which can positively change your life around. Therefore, how could that be negative? How could you come to realize that you have abilities or characteristics that you may have only hinted at before be bad? How can learning about other people who share similar attributes with you be dangerous? Man, in the general way of saying man, meaning women and men, make evil, evil. Remember fear spreads. Forget the fact that without the sun, life would not exist in the same manner as it does now. Forget the moon's impact on our marine life. Forget that the ancient pyramids, which still stand today, were constructed in alignment with the stars. Forget the use of the stars as a way to grow crops and navigate the seas. Forget learning about your Self, just focus on learning about others.

I believe it was a few days after returning from my trip and just prior to me beginning to write this book that I discovered people with my particular "Signs" are often writers. Now look. Lack of knowledge is the only real answer to anyone who opposes getting to know their Self. Astrology is not to be written off no matter how educated or spiritually advanced you feel you are. Seeing how you are required to learn about forefathers and ancient rulers, then you should you be able to learn about your Self as well.

OPEN FOR BUSINESS

Icannot stress enough how important it will be that you open your Self up to ideas that come from your brothers and sisters in your future. You should always take an idea into consideration and look for even the smallest use it could provide. You should always listen to another's idea and avoid putting them down or making them feel less than for offering up a way. That is, as long as that idea is appropriate and not off color. Remember you are building a future. Therefore, you must be a leader of some sort. So as a leader you do not want to alienate your Self from potential help. Now, keep in mind as you begin to open up and discover your true Self, information will naturally begin to come to you. This "data" will come from different places at different times. How you react to these occurrences will be essential. You see, once you begin to communicate the vision for your future you will attract others who can help you achieve your goals. Study the law of attraction and the law of compensation for further insight into why keeping an open mind is essential to your future's progress. Information may come from friends or associates, or it may come while you walk down the street. You may even overhear a conversation amongst people you have never met and will never see again. It is up to you to recognize these "messages" and put them to proper use. You will not always know from where or when they are coming, but as time moves on you will soon realize why they are coming.

Another method of opening up to others' ideas is by learning about culture and cultural differences. Learning to respect differences will decide the unity your future possesses. Upon removing levels of conditioning, this should become easier to achieve. Remember to show understanding and patience to those with backgrounds and customs that differ from you. This is essential because it breaks down barriers such as race and class. This breakdown will also help in shedding more fear and old thinking. This will further improve understanding and communication between one another in your future. Your patience will show on your face, in your body language, and be heard in your words. Remember, the tiniest gesture or reaction can transform the thoughts of thousands. Negativity alienates, and at times it does so without even being verbally communicated. Therefore, you can be felt as easily as you can be heard.

Remember, if you are putting down another for their perceived lack, you may be very well telling on yourself, admitting outwardly and openly that you your Self are lacking

SOCIETY

"Little children, you are from God and have conquered them; for the one
who is in you is greater than the one who is in the world"
Jesus of Nazareth

You need to understand and be able to recognize how society sees you and has conditioned you. This mold will continue to take shape if you do not break free. You also need to discover why society wants to condition you. Know that society works hand in hand with shaping your Ego. We have discussed conditioning prior to now and you should be hopefully learning to recognize the vast amount of it that lies in your Self and others around you. Conditioning happens daily, hourly, and by the minute. You can and have become conditioned without even knowing it is happening to you. Most of it is sent to you through the media and subliminal messaging. Society dictates this conditioning one way or another. This hold that society will place on you will become your thoughts, words and actions. After time these new thoughts, words, and actions will become natural. This conditioning will now appear as a way to identify and/or label your Self. You can easily get lost doing this. Soon material "things" will have extreme importance to you. These "things" will soon define you rather than your personal accomplishments. The "out" will become more important than the "in." Ideas such as status and image can become important to your everyday life. You can become susceptible to following trends and can be easily influenced by the latest and greatest "whatever" that comes along. Society will shape what you buy and how much you are willing to spend for your "stuff." You may look to others amongst you and attempt to copy or idolize them. You will get a steady dose of this form of influence from particular genres of music, television, and the world of fashion. Some music will say to you, "you are not cool" or popular enough. That is, of course, unless you are living in a similar manner to the "artist" who is portraying the lifestyle you are hearing about in their songs. Magazines will tell women they should look a certain way to feel good about their appearance. The media will create huge stories out of nothing to help boost ratings. Entertainers and athletes will have a way of making you feel less then. You will attempt to keep up with them instead of focusing on you and your family's real needs. This does not always happen purposely, but nonetheless it happens. Now, I would like to stop here and say that I am personally not against achieving financial wealth. I am not against the desire to own nice "things." I happen to love automobiles and nice clothing. I feel it is important to feel good about your appearance and present your Self with pride in that appearance. However, I am against being greedy and misleading people. I am against some of the behaviors associated with these "things" you and I deem important in society. I am against obtaining this wealth by negative actions such as manipulating others. I am against the senseless behavior the non-entertainer and non-athlete displays while trying to obtain the status the actual entertainer and athlete has. I am against being a slave to money and "things." I am against the "out" speaking for you before the "in" is heard.

The television tells you what to buy and who to buy it from. Then it tells you who is and who is not important. It tells you, the same "you" which I alluded to earlier, who is full of power and beauty, that you have become too fat, too slow, too poor. When you finally turn off the television, then your magazine makes you believe aging is unnatural and ugly. We as people have become so focused on items, trends, and statuses that we are now lost. This takes us further away from our Self and helps to develop that other self. Perhaps we feel "cooler" or more important with more items? Maybe we feel more attractive or sexier following a trend? Your Ego loves every minute of confusion you are feeding your Self. These thoughts may feel natural but this is an error. These will be some of your toughest choices to make in finding your future. What are you willing to give up and disassociate from? Are you sure you want to give up the same materials that your friends keep?

While you are here you should enjoy your Self and what the world has to offer. However, you should do so while remaining humble and fully aware of your Ego. You should be aware that your house will not be your house one day. Just as your car will not be your car. You should be aware of what you are seeing and hearing on a daily basis. You should be equally aware of what a healthy dose of this will lead to in your future. Understanding this form of conditioning is essential for you in order to develop your future the proper way.

Remove your Self from the control society has placed on you. Not only does society want you to follow along without telling you where you are truly headed, it frowns upon you breaking free and beginning to lead your own way. While it desperately needs free thinkers it does not breed free thinkers. Society breeds workers. Society breeds sheep and cattle, not lions and birds. While workers will always be necessary in order to achieve mass production, regardless of your product, you should encourage your new society to breed lions and birds. Birds symbolize freedom, lions symbolize leadership. Free thinking is freedom. Leadership is freedom. Self-control is freedom. Allow the people in your future the chance to think and live with quality. Allow your future the opportunity to rid itself from any and all negative energy. Celebrate and reward your workers, or the trappings of greed, isolation, and more will undoubtedly have a negative impact on you both directly and indirectly.

Society is not only the television you watch, the magazines you read, and the music you hear. Society is your parents, family, and friends. Society is your associates, your school, your jobs, and your groups. Understand this, because just as society is conditioning you, it is also conditioning everyone else around you. Society is everywhere; therefore its branches are too. By now there is no way you have not been exposed. Race relations in the West from centuries ago have impacted those who occupy the Earth in the present. Religious claims and beliefs from B.C. are still alive in A.D. This is included to show you just how much and how far thought and action can travel. Your job now is to find the right kind of conditioning. Become conditioned to kindness, to honor, and friendship. Become conditioned to forgiveness and compassion, to healthy habits, and self-education. Become shaped by the greatness and success in your Self and in others. Become familiar with the Source within you. The goal is for you to condition you. You must take action to counteract the action being taken against you. You do this by gaining control of your Self. You do this by telling your Self what to think and how to feel. You do this by making your own label, one free of Ego, but full of love and truth. The rewards will be endless.

Remember when questioning, analyzing, and recognizing, that you should do so with love and out of the need to grow and shed. While you may not be happy with everything you will find, this is not reason to become distant from your family and friends, and your true Self. This is where love must come into play

MIND OVER MATTER

*"We cannot solve our problems with the same thinking
we used when we created them"*
Albert Einstein

By now you should know that I believe our Source wants you to be happy and enjoy your time here on Earth. By now you should know that I believe our Source wants you to be full of love and compassion. As do I know our Source wants you to be full of positive energy and maintain an undoubting belief in your Self and your abilities. What you may not be aware of though, is that I believe our Source would want you to achieve success and wealth. However, the success and wealth does not necessarily mean money and status. I am sure our Source does not relate to man-made concepts as likely as it relates to the personal growth within you. The growth we achieve in our hearts and minds is success and wealth. Acquiring knowledge is success and wealth. Now, there is a direct connection to success and financial wealth in individuals who attain great levels of personal growth. However, that aspect is not the direct aim of this writing. On the topic of financial wealth I suggest you read the numerous books written and published by the profound writer and thinker Napoleon Hill. His teachings will provide more of a direct aim in developing the tools for financial success. His book ***Think and Grow Rich*** is a blueprint for wealth and more. This writing aims to help you achieve personal growth by ridding you of negative conditioning and establishing new habits and form. Simplified, this writing aims to recondition you while simultaneously redirecting your future. Money has no value in the aim of this writing, and we will leave the subject of currency alone. Truthfully I did not receive one single message about money and its importance in your future. Helping your sisters and brothers is money to me. Educating your Self and discovering truth is wealth to us. Success that continues to build every time you help someone else, and then that someone helps someone who in turn helps themselves - this is what we are looking to establish, this is success to us. The wealth that truth provides you with is not the type of wealth anyone can ever take away from you. Just as it is not the type of wealth you can ever lose by sharing it with others. These are the messages I received and was moved to write about. This success and wealth I speak of is forever, and never for the moment like the potential that money and status offers if not achieved and managed properly. In your future, place a value on the wealth and success you acquire by growing within your Self first and foremost. Do this regardless of the money you may or may not acquire. I am sorry to inform you, but money and status will not enrich you and your future the way love and forgiveness will. Money and status will not enrich you the way empowering your mind, heart, and soul will. I know this will discourage some of you. Some of you will undoubtedly disagree with this message, but this is true. Status in particular is perception. Status can change faster than the clock on the wall does, so why chase some "thing" so elusive? However, some of you will undoubtedly attain status in your future. You will be looked upon as great men and women. You will become leaders who are innovators and decision makers. These perceptions of you could be exact and you may feel a strong sense of accomplishment from this discovery. This is fine, for having a fondness of your Self because you have achieved greatness is appropriate. Do not believe anyone who says different. However, upon achieving this status, be able to recognize the truth in your Self and do not fall victim to your own hype. In essence, just be honest with your Self. It will be easy to become cocky or arrogant when men shout your name in celebration. It will be much easier to become full of the "other" you. You should know what is true and what is not true when being spoken about. You would be wise to not become too attached to the perception others have of you, allowing it to define you. Doing this will only serve to feed your Ego and blur the proper vision needed to find your future. You should remain humble and thankful for the praise you receive. Always remember that greatness lies in the next man or woman as well, and the only difference at the moment is that you have already tapped into your supply. While you are reading this they could be on their way to joining you, and for you and your future's sake, I hope they are. The phrase "all men were created equal" is true. However, where a change occurs is when conditioning starts and some realize their potential, while others do not. Understand there is another "you". Not a "you", for you are unique, so rather a someone somewhere with a great idea, plan, or calling, just like you. The state of your future will depend upon you allowing others the chance to realize the same "shine" you have or are after. You should never hold them back out of fear, doubt, insecurity, or hate. The more people you have contributing positively in your future, the better your future will become. No matter how great a man or woman becomes, they should realize greatness has been here before them and will be here after them. Meaning yes, celebrate tonight, but tomorrow morning get up and give thanks. I would like to remind you that in no way am I stating you should live financially poor. I am stating though there are more important goals in life. Deeds outweigh money every time. Money comes and goes, yet your deeds can stick around and transcend forever. You get to take your soul with you. The money stays behind. Therefore, it may be wise to place more importance on your soul than on your bank accounts.

*The Source wants you to possess a combination of Self-motivation mixed in with a willingness to help. Once you get to the top of the ladder, hold it for the next person who is climbing up. Your Source wants you to find courage and possess a strong focus on finding truth, but once discovering and doing so, you are to teach others how to do the same *

UNIQUE OR DIE

"Imitation is suicide"
Ralph Waldo Emerson

Your future will begin to prosper the more you and your brothers and sisters become unique. There should not be any "copying" in your future. However, do not confuse this statement as reason to ignore the work and foundation your sisters and brothers have already laid down for you. Do not confuse this as a reason to not learn and practice the methods and principles that are available to you. Meaning if you want to become a great athlete you should watch and study other great athletes. However, there is a difference between studying athletes' techniques and methods, and imitating them. Imitation is foreign to your essence. You must find your own greatness, and bring "you" out for the world to see. There is already one of them; where are "you" though? Your future will look less like my past the more you understand and then apply this principle.

Stop going along with every trend or style. Only follow a trend or style if you truly like that style or trend for you. Find a way to incorporate it into your personal style and make it unique to you. Try going style-less sometimes. Style-less is still a style, right?

A WARNING TO THE WISE

"To enjoy good health, to bring happiness to one's family, to bring peace to all,
one must first discipline and control one's own mind. If man can control
his mind he can find way to Enlightenment, and all wisdom and
virtue will naturally come to him".
Buddha

Some of you will advance in building your personal futures faster than your sisters and brothers will. At times it will seem easy to become frustrated and upset with them because of their inconsistency or lack of motivation and progress. Instead of getting upset, try to use your power of understanding and love when looking at them. Try to help them. We have discussed the need for your future to be in harmony, so attempting to help another person is more than appropriate. However, if they reject your help by ignoring you, feeding off of you, or by showing you an unwillingness to help themselves, then move forward without them. Moving on without them is essential for your growth, for you do not have the easiest task ahead of you in creating your future. Do not allow someone to feed off you. If they are in need they can possibly eat with you, but not off of you. Now, when you move forward, speak lovingly and truthfully to them. Explain your reason for moving forward. Attempt to assure them that you may be waiting for them if they do begin to move forward too. Remember standing still is unacceptable. From time to time you may check on them, but do not allow them to prevent you from doing what you set out to do. The emotional connection to your friends and family may make it difficult to do what I am proposing. This emotional connection will prevent you from capturing the necessary progress you will need. The love you have for them must have a filter at times. Find the necessary balance. This discovery is essential.

WOMEN

"Since we all came from a woman, got our name from a woman and our game
from a woman; I wonder why we take from our women, why we rape our
women, do we hate our women"?
Tupac Shakur

At this time I would like to explain the extreme importance women will play in the development of your future. In my humble opinion, the value of women has been downplayed severely in my past, and this tragedy should not continue. In your future, women should return to their proper place in the minds of men and, more importantly, in the minds of women. Gone should be the days of women being viewed as less than men. Understand that a woman, whether in nature or in human form, has the ability to give birth and to create life. This should be all you really need to know and understand to place an extreme value on her. Do "Mother Earth" and "Mother Nature" sound familiar? I believe Africa is looked at as the place of man's origin. Africa is known as the "Mother-land", is it not? Possibly the "Mother-ship" or "Mother-board" rings a bell? Life cannot exist without a mother, a woman, who was once a girl. Women have so much power here on Earth, and yet some of them and some of the men who interact with them do not tap into that power. I am not positive of why or how it was decided that men were greater than women other than the obvious answer which is that, men said that men were. Maybe it has to do with the idea that God is a man or is due to the religious story of Adam and Eve? I am unsure to be completely honest. I am not sure why women were not allowed voting rights or equal pay in the workplace either. Just as I am unsure how in other species the woman is at times the stronger, fiercer, more reliable parent or hunter, but in our species, women have been placed behind men rather than next to them. The essence of the woman in society has been kept a secret and downplayed. The power they possess has become dormant. Honestly women have the ability to make a man who and what he is, and also what he is not. Allow me to pause right here and assure the men that I am aware we are fully capable of attaining success on our own. However, women have often played a momentous role in shaping and completing powerful, successful men. Whether she is a mother, friend, girlfriend, or a wife, a woman can single-handedly give a man the love, comfort, and support that only she can offer him. Some men believe that a woman's place is in the home or in service to him. Some women agree with this. I need not agree or disagree. I simply hope that the man values his woman in this role, just as I hope the woman values her Self in it too.

This was not written to create a debate about whether a man or woman is better suited or more capable for the completion of a job or role. This, however, was written to empower women. This was created to show men that if they think a woman is beneath them, or anything less than an equal, then they are thinking out of Ego and pure ignorance. So God, our Source, values men more than women? At one time I thought differently about the "order" of men and women. Truth is, there is no order; only roles, qualities, and characteristics, as well as conditioning and environment. Is your mother not worthy of the same respect as your father because she is second in the "order", though first to display love and compassion? Wait; let us not forget the precious order. Some of these questions may sound silly but I will continue. Was Martin Luther King, Jr. only fighting for the equal rights of black men? Was Jesus excluding women with his message of love and consciousness? I am confused because I thought we were all "God's" children. So "he" has favorites? This is quite amusing to me so please forgive the assumed notice of my sarcasm.

To any man who may have a hard time reading this, you are either insecure or feel threatened by empowered women. What's more, you must have never been intimate with a woman who is in tune with her Self at some level. When I say intimate I mean by its truest definition. This must be true if you doubt the power she is capable of. In addition, there are qualities in men that only come from a woman. It is time for men to build women up and overstand that when doing so, they are also committing to building themselves up. Women, in your future please believe in yourselves and the abilities you possess. Please believe how important you are to life's survival. Stop settling for men who do not value you and your essential existence. At the same time, value and respect your Self. Please stop allowing yourselves to look unladylike. Please stop feeling justified for doing less than you should because of the way men act or "make" you act. Your Source made you, therefore do not allow a man to define you. You were made with qualities that even the greatest and most successful men cannot possess without you. You are natural nurturers, lovers, and caretakers; you are natural providers, defenders, and protectors. Therefore, you are natural leaders. Please know this and strive to not only improve yourselves, but strive to use your gifts to improve the men who share the land with you. So as your future evolves, powerful women must be in the forefront of its development. This positioning is essential.

Understand who and where you come from. Understand your environment. Your environment is everywhere you are. Understand how it shapes and conditions you. After gaining that understanding of your environment, love it. Love it because whether good or bad, you can now grow from it

NEW NORMS

In your future, strive to educate the masses on material like this that has been placed before you. Work to make these lessons and truths the norm in your society. The norms I am speaking of are natural actions and reactions. In doing so, soon every human being can be offered the proper enlightenment to lead them towards their true potential. There is a big difference between thinking and knowing. Make an effort to show people you know the truth. You do this by setting an example. You set this example by not allowing or waiting for a destructive emotion like fear to prevent you from becoming the truth you now know. You can accomplish this by the way you think, the way you talk, and by the way you carry your Self. Even how you greet your fellow man can leave a lasting impression. Like attracts like. You get back what you give out. Meaning if you disrespect others, others will disrespect you in some way at some point in your life. You can start establishing what tomorrow will look like today.

Show others they can and should set an example too. This can be done without speaking a word. The more people you have establishing these new norms for others to take notice of, the more others will begin to set their own example, and so on and so on. This will occur regardless of your choice to either set a positive or a negative example. This is conditioning again. If you place me in a home where it is appropriate to yell and curse when there are "problems", it is highly likely I will think it is appropriate to yell and curse as a way to solve my problems outside of that home. We all have a great responsibility to one another. Often we do not realize this. The responsibility exists because we are all connected to one another. Someone is always watching you. Remember this and remember your future is at stake.

THE TIGHTROPE

"Notice that the stiffest tree is most easily cracked, while the
bamboo or willow survives while bending with the wind"
Bruce Lee

Looking back at what I have been exposed and now conditioned to, I would like to share a belief I personally live with. My personal philosophy is to live life as balanced as possible. This approach can be applied in all walks of life, from the food you eat to the activities you enjoy. It allows you to never become so deeply involved that you end up missing out. Just as balance will allow you to become well rounded and more welcoming to life's mysteries, it will also afford you a healthy understanding of others' backgrounds and lifestyles. This balance will prevent you from harming your Self from too much indulgence. It will allow your mind to stay open to new opportunities and change. Bruce Lee's martial arts "style" was made up of numerous variations of fighting and combat. He created a balance, and thus created a new style. When learning truth, I believe it is essential to do so with balance. The world has offered many ideas, solutions, reasons, and "truths". Some of these "findings", however, are simply not true. They will be delivered to you as a truth but are far from that which they appear. Often a person's perception of an event, time, or message will appear as a fact. So this may be true for them but does not mean it has to be true for you. I have watched the world and experienced life, but I am far from being done with my journey and do not qualify as a master or "expert" on what is best for everyone in this vast world. The words in this writing are now my truth. Some of this truth I searched for, while most of it was sent to me. What was sent to me was delivered because I opened my Self up to receive. This came to be because I allowed it to be. You will not find your way without looking for the path. Accepting everything put in front of you will not allow you to search. I found my path by maintaining a balance, meaning not all my truth came from one person, one place or one "thing". By closing my Self off and simply diving into one source of information, I would have become just that one piece of information. Where am I in that? Where are others who are not in that? What have I found? The answer is little to nothing. You cannot truly find something that was purposely placed there to be seen.

Besides the truth my experiences, family, and friends have offered me, I have gained knowledge from numerous religions, ideologies, and philosophies. I have gathered from Jesus but also from Buddha. I have listened and learned from the Dali Lama, Marcus Aurelius, and Ralph Waldo Emerson. I am presently learning from Mohammed, Epictetus and Malcolm X. I have learned from strict dogma and Mother Earth, just as I have learned from film and music. I gained insight from both elders and children and grasped just as much from students as I have from teachers. All and more have helped develop the path for me. As I previously wrote, a lot of these truths were presented to me almost like puzzle pieces. It was then my duty to find how they all pieced together. This knowledge that was presented to me came from various places, people, and times. I reached this point in my life, which is completing this writing, by developing a healthy balance of experience and truth and then allowing life to reinforce it time and time again as a way of self-regulating. I did this by paying attention to my actions, thoughts, and feelings. I did this by questioning my Self as to how I feel and think after a situation occurs. This writing, if you read the foreword, came to me, just like much of the knowledge in it came to me. What I am attempting to tell you regarding you and the potential to build your future the way that you want it, has been proven in these very pages you are reading. This writing is proof that the principles presented here work when applied and continuously practiced. If you knew me growing up you would know that this was hardly the way I saw my future going as a young child, or as a young man for that matter. Surely writing a book would not provide me with the lifestyle I once believed I or my family required. Writing a book surely would not satisfy my motivation to succeed nor was it my plan. However, it has, and sometimes there are plans other than your own in the works for you. In my eyes, this book is the most important contribution I have made to the world outside of creating a child. The way this book came about is something no one needs to believe in, but if wise they will. Equally it is an experience no one can ever take away from me. This text is proof that greatness is alive and available to anyone who refuses to give up searching for it, provided they maintain an undeniable and unshaken belief that no matter how unrecognizable, it is destined for them.

If "God" lives in all of us then all of us offer up God to be seen. If all man's intentions were just then maybe it would be wise to gather all knowledge and truth from one source and never question or search for further understanding. However, it is not, and therefore it should not be the only method of finding the "way". If God did not intend on being used by more than one person then life would be a shell of its present self. Remember truth is contagious and is designed to be shared, regardless of where and what it comes from

FAIRY TALES DO COME TRUE

"It's not living that matters, but rather living rightly"
Socrates

Many people believe that there is no way "something" like this writing can be sent to someone. So naturally the "truth" that I believe in cannot be real. That lack of belief is one of the major reasons why we are presently divided as a people. Not to mention everyone has a different truth, a different belief, and while this difference should be healthy, sadly it has become reason to divide instead of unite. It has also become reason to point the finger and judge. And even sadder is that many of us are extremely outward and negative when sharing what we believe to be the "truth". If you know something to be the truth, then there is no real reason to become negative when your belief is challenged, questioned, or met with confusion. If your truth is pure and righteous, what room does negativity occupy when discussing what you feel or know to be the truth? If you are so right, then why become angry when discussing your views? The person who is "wrong" should be the one who gets upset, if anyone must. You will hopefully learn that often we are either all right or all wrong. I do not believe for a second that our Source argues, fights, or hates. Hence, we should make the best attempt to avoid doing so as well. This is included to show that there is no real need to tell someone they are wrong in their beliefs as long as those beliefs are not imposed on you or harming others. The need to tell others they are wrong will often produce anger and separation. In your future you must strive to come together. This is not an easy accomplishment but it is the proper reaction if you come from a "higher power" or understand the way to salvation in even the smallest portion. Direct your anger instead of it directing you. Anger, like separation, clouds the mind. The truth clears the mind. You will not find the truth without walking a path so why would you want to cloud the journey? Therefore, find a way to communicate that creates a union rather than the alternative or your real future will remain dormant.

This should be easy for some of you to pick up and follow because we speak the same language. For the others, you are still learning the language I am speaking, but seeing how we are from the same tribe, the same village, the more you experience life, the language you have yet learned will start to become understandable. The truths you do not fully grasp at this time will come back to you and echo throughout your being one day soon. We all find our way differently, at different times, through different mediums. However, I know, almost like a sixth sense, that for a lot of you, if you look into your hearts, minds, and souls, you will soon find that this information makes sense and you will be able to relate to this writing right away

THE WORLD IS YOURS

"Up, you mighty race, accomplish what you will"
Marcus Garvey

Look at the history of your Self, your family, and the world around you. Doing so will hopefully offer insight into what you are lacking in order to create a better future. Look at how people in the past interacted and settled issues. Take notice of how people treat one another and the value that has been placed on human life here. Give your attention to their mistakes and strive to improve upon them. Be aware of how the political system is set up and has functioned in the past. Survey the financial system in your nation and analyze it to see if there could be improvements made. Amend these mistakes so that your future does not repeat the trappings of our past. Examine ex-leaders and while noting their positive contributions, also notice the errors they made and strive to not only absorb their genius, but to learn from their shortcomings. For once again, the past should be used as a learning tool in any and every way possible. From events, to the evolution of man and their role in shaping what we now call the present, the past offers much needed insight to shape the future. There is much to learn from previous life on our planet. Failing to do so will be detrimental to you and your future. Look at the Earth and its resources. Ask your Self if there is any way to improve upon the use of these precious gifts. Evaluate the education system and ask, is there something missing? Cease from going along with everything people have said, written, and established. Lose the sheep syndrome that so many have developed to follow "whatever" is put in front of them. Stop accepting everything that comes your way that you do not like. Stop being distracted by meaningless "things" and events. We will not sit by and allow you to continue to suffer at the hands of others who are attempting to stifle the love that lies in each and every one of us. We will not sit by without attempting to help you better your Self. We will not accept the norm and challenge you to no longer accept it either. These others have continuously demonstrated a lower level of being that separates, destroys the whole, and rewards only a few. These others must not be able to continue to hold down, push aside, and control the masses.

We urge you to come together in your future and become leery of anyone and anything that preaches the opposite of that movement.

Why not give "you" a chance? Why not start telling your Self what to think, what to believe, what to feel, and what to do? Why not be in control? Why not find your truth? Why not decide your life, your future? Why not find your purpose, your "job", your path? Why not create your future instead of accepting the one you believe awaits you? Why is a question you have a right to ask

YOUR MOVE

I am practically pleading with you to change the world for the better, but only if you feel a change is indeed required. A change is needed from where we stand whether you believe it or not. If and when you agree with our assessment, know that the change will not come about in an easy manner. You cannot simply tell someone to read this or listen to that. You cannot proclaim how you have found the answer to a better world, and how they too will soon realize this new world after experiencing what you have recently discovered. Not everyone will get "it" or understand "it", and you as the student must also be careful before you try to become a teacher. There is a big difference between verbal and non-verbal teaching. Verbal teaching, since word is so powerful, requires preparation and extreme self-focus to ensure you are saying the proper messages. You are, however, qualified to teach non-verbally right away. You can show others the need for a change when leading by example. You can demonstrate the need for change by establishing order in your life. You can display your greatness without saying a word, for non-verbal communication speaks volumes. To those of you who will need to verbally teach, you should learn that the word is life, as we have established and seen. We will, rather you will, need to spread the message that a future built off of love and honor, compassion and truth, is under way, and you are one of its spokes people. You will know when your time to speak is upon you, and we believe you will be outstanding when doing so.

*Nowhere in this writing will you find me attempting to discourage you from having fun, becoming financially successful or enjoying a particular lifestyle that you may have become accustomed to or are interested in living. Nor will you find me attempting to persuade you to abandon your beliefs. You do not need to follow the message in this writing, for you have been given free will. The choice has always been yours. I know many of you will reject this writing because it

William Autore - Finding Your Future

challenges your way of living. This challenges the way you make your money, the way you find pleasure, and your level of comfort. All your wants and perceived needs will be challenged. For others this writing will challenge your beliefs. I will sound like an enemy to your establishment. Just know that you have been given a way out of the confusion some of you are surrounded by, a way out of the chaos some of you are immensely soaked in. The choice is yours and will always be waiting there for you to grab onto if you decide to let go*

THE PROCESS IS ETERNAL

"A man of genius makes no mistakes; his errors are
volitional and are the portals to discovery"
James Joyce

T his writing is not the final answer, and some of the levels you begin to operate on after reading this are not the final levels to ascend to and rest on. This writing can and should be used as a bridge. This bridge is here to take you to another teaching, another lesson, and another experience. Soon only your thoughts and feelings will matter. Soon I will not be in the present with you. Therefore, I leave you this as a tool to use to better your Self and the world that awaits you. You have a responsibility not only to your real Self but to those who are yet to come to Earth. You may not agree with this view of your responsibilities. This is fine, just make sure you reevaluate your Self if this concept seems odd to you.

While the individual is the focus, its scope is paired with how each individual can benefit the whole. If you agree with this perspective, then your responsibility to those who have left is also required - these individuals who passed on with hopes that one day the change they wanted to see and attempted to get across to us would become a reality. Their reality is now in your hands. There may seem to be some sort of "pressure" on you in holding this responsibility. There is none, because pressure is nothing until you allow it to become "something". Always remember that while you have a responsibility to those who have come before you and to those who are yet to arrive, you also have a responsibility to your Self. You owe it to your Self first and foremost to become properly conditioned. Without taking care of your Self it will be harder to take care of others. For this is what those before you who were enlightened understood and, in essence, are asking of you now. You see, they knew the potential you possess. They knew the real Self, the Source that lives in you. Your responsibility is not necessary to complete a project or theory from a former leader or old soul twice removed. It is, however, your responsibility to realize the wonder in you the way they realized it in them. Do this and create your method for achieving the greatness that is reserved for you. All the while establish your present, and most importantly your future. Understand that this development will take time and you may "fail" repeatedly. Do not be discouraged because no one is judging you for your "failure". Know that often there is more of a lesson in losing than in winning. Greatness takes time to develop. Enlightenment may take years to achieve. This is why you have heard these types of statements several times throughout the writing, because the process of change is a process. Success will feel unattainable to the majority of you at some time during your life. We promise you that this feeling is normal for you and your time here on Earth. However, the wise thought is that this negative feeling will soon pass, for it is ultimately not natural to your essence. Soon enough you will overcome your feelings of hopelessness and doubt if you wish to. Hold on to your goals and dreams, and most importantly, hold onto your "real" Self. Be smarter than so many in the past who have allowed their Selves to get lost in a sea of confusion and chaos due to Ego and false conditioning. Be smarter than to go along with those around you now who have displayed inappropriate frequencies and vibrations. Be smarter than to fall victim to being less than the greatness that lives in you.

You are special. Some of you knew this long before ever finding this book. Some of you have come to realize this now after reading this writing, while others may still need some time. Nevertheless, all of you are. It is time to put that "special" to the test. Now is good. Understand that greatness does not copy. Therefore, there are levels and variations to it. For some, being honorable and raising a family to live the same is greatness. This is a tremendous feat, and those of you who find this future are celebrated. For others, greatness may look like a leader of a movement or cause. For a small percentage of you, greatness will be seen in your loss. Therefore, greatness is available to any and everyone who searches for its unlimited branches.

I SHINE, YOU SHINE

"Our prime purpose in life is to help others.
If you can't help them, at least don't hurt them"
His Holiness, the 14th Dalai Lama

Y ou must decide what kind of individual you want to be because your decision will not only affect you, your family, and friends, but your decision will affect others' families and friends. Believe this; it is your world but it is your neighbor's world too. Whether you want to argue it or not, we are all connected. Just as we affect one another, we affect the trees, the oceans, the animals, and the frequency of the Earth. For you see, as intellectual as you are or believe you are, learn quickly that we are all united, somehow, someway. An example of this can be seen in the old belief that the world was flat. People thought and believed this at one time. All it took was for one person to start the rumor and it spread. So how can we not be connected? If you tell me the Earth is flat and I take your word then are we not connected at least in thought and belief? Lose your Ego and the false belief system you and others have created for you as soon as possible. Realize that you are not supposed to be separated from one another and from "God". The more you are wrongly conditioned, the more separated you become. We are not to be separated from our Source's nature, which is love and compassion. These connections are essential to our nature which is one in the same with our Source. The more you are wrongly conditioned, the more wrongly conditioned you make others. We need more love in this world. We do not need more hate, separation, and fear, for it is not "Godly" to act in such a manner. In case you are still unaware, you are "Godly". You are an extension of "God", so appropriateness is required. This will take time to develop but the rewards are eternal.

A REMINDER OF SORTS

"Change is the law of life. And those who look only to the past or
present are certain to miss the future."
John F. Kennedy

Once again, you are going to stumble while deciding
your future. My favorite quote at the moment is "It is human to err,
but it is divine to forgive". So at once, forgive your Self for the errors
you have made and will undoubtedly make moving forward. Now
forgive your neighbor, and then forgive your so-called "enemies".
Act as divinely as possible, as often as possible. Fill your mind with
love and purpose and watch how much happier you will become.
Learn to let go, and watch what you end up getting to hold on to.
Look around at the people who may be truly mistreating you. If your
perception is correct then realize that they very well may need help.
Understand that there is something wrong with them, not you. There
is a lack in them, not you. For in reality, they are mistreating
themselves if they are mistreating you. Do not take everything
personal in your future either. Understand the previous statement and
you should be able to "deal" with them and anyone else who you may
negatively encounter a little easier.

At times we expect people to "know better". We especially
expect this from adults. This is an error, largely due to our
perception. While I do agree it is natural to feel that adults should
know better, many adults are not in their right mind. As a child,
attempt to understand this and show the adult more understanding
and love because they could very well require more of it than you do.
Just because you are a youth does not mean you cannot be more
right-minded than an adult. Just because you are young does not
mean you cannot start today, right now, in mapping out your future.
Sooner is always better. Adults, allow the children around you the
chance to dream and find their own paths. Do this even if their path
is different from the one you feel is best suited. Some will disagree
with this belief but as long as the child is guided in the right
direction, meaning that child has the proper respect, education, and
love instilled in them, then they are equipped for their journey

regardless of the chosen route. Understand that this child is an individual and should be allowed to be one within your boundaries. This individual, while undoubtedly "made up" of the traits and characteristics they got from you, at heart, is still an individual. They will need the freedom of finding themselves for themselves. You should help foster a positive, loving, and intelligent environment for them to find their future. Help them do this under your guidance, not your command.

EXODUS

"Let the future tell the truth, and evaluate each one according to
his work and accomplishments. The present is theirs; the future,
for which I have really worked, is mine"
Nikola Tesla

W hy stress over something that does not require stress? Wait, why stress at all? Why fight if not for freedom or a better way of life? Why be negative? Are these behaviors needed on a daily basis if they are not creating a positive? I do not wish to confuse anyone following along by implying I have never stressed, fought or been negative. Nor do I wish to sound naive in assuming that neither of us will ever have a bad day throughout the remainder of our lives. It is not always easy to control our behavior. However, what I am asking of you is to ask your Self, can you improve upon your attitude, outlook, and day in, day out mind set? Can you smile more? Can you find beauty in Nature instead of a "thing" with monetary value? Can you control your anger and stress by searching for the source of it and learning what triggers your reactions? Can you then understand that you now have a choice in how you deal with the situation? Can you now see a glimpse of your power, your ability, and your potential? Understanding your Self provides control and knowledge. If you know stress can cause health issues, then why continue to allow it to find its way into your life? What is more important than your health? If you understand the power anger has over our lives, why allow your Self to become angry for "nothing"? Why become upset at such meaningless and temporary things? Why become bothered and then stressed over a "thing" you cannot control? Why waste the precious time and energy? Why allow so much of nothing to matter? There is a lack if you are easily moved to emotion by "things". If you have not yet realized you make "nothing" into "something", please do so now.

I am also fully aware of the emotions that come along with the desire to lead or be a part of a cause. Examples such as a revolution or demonstration apply. Such situations will demand anger and stress at times. So if these emotions are required, they should only be to bring about a change for the betterment of the whole. I suggest researching Gene Sharp for methods of peaceful revolutionary tactics. I also suggest finding a way to channel your emotions in the right direction. Your future will require a revolution of sorts because the present conditions are unacceptable for the whole. This revolution begins and ends with you as an individual. If we have enough people leading a "Self" revolution, then there will be less of a need for a mass revolution. You see, I would like to forget about the current state of the world and the potential issues undoubtedly awaiting you. Yet these issues will threaten your future if a change is not brought about, so forgetting them would be irresponsible and dangerous. Not making attempts to help you rid the world of those issues would be out of character.

Now I began this writing attempting to explain to you that I saw your future. The future I saw for you was not the future it should be. I do not wish to paint an unrealistic picture of the world at the time of this writing. There is much work to be done, and at times a change seems impossible. There have been many years of conditioning and lack of growth, which has made the present quite confusing and chaotic. Moving forward, I am acting on faith. This choice comes from a trust and a knowledge of the divine. I am also acting on the belief that you will use this material to better your Self and others. This belief I share is the belief that you will make the right decisions moving forward in your life. However, this principle needs to be yours; for my belief will only carry us so far.

I do not know if you will accept the truth that is in these pages. This uncertainty occupying me is largely due to the nature of the world you now live in. This "task" requires belief, focus, and time. This challenge requires strength, persistence, trust, and love. You will not reach your destination unless you continuously search for knowledge and enlightenment. I am unsure if this is attainable for all of you who will journey into this writing. The law of averages and several other forces will eliminate a large number of you from even finding the material written here. A larger number of you simply will not care. Others will find the material but continue to be controlled and believe in what the next person said either presently or some time ago, finding that their word is much easier to believe and grasp than the word written here. There is not as much work to do when "someone" or "something" else decides for you. The lack of motivation is comforting to most. These facts and reasoning remove my expectations of an outcome. I know what I hope and wish for, but I will remain "realistic" in my position and in my view of the world until more join me. I want for you to discover the power you have and refuse to give up and give in. I have repeated my goal for you and my requests for change several times now. Stressing it should show you the extreme importance I place on the tasks before you. The need for a change is evident all around us, but who will be brave enough to take on the challenge of finding their true Self? Who will be brave enough to shed what has become normal for our race here on this planet? Which one of you will lead the world in a different direction, one that leads towards love, prosperity, and righteousness for all? Which one of you will decide "I am powerful enough to choose my future"? When will you say "I no longer like what I see in my Self, my community, my World"? When will you say "enough is enough" and decide to no longer be under control, but rather be in control? Yes, you have been controlled, and I hope this bothers you enough to take the words in this writing seriously. I hope it bothers you enough that you find your way back to your essence where you rightfully belong. The real you eagerly awaits your return.

It will be easy to not believe in these words and truths, but ask your Self why that is. Is it due to my status or background? Is it because the television did not introduce us to one another? Is it because I am operating outside of the norm? Or is it due to the fact that we have become a skeptical race of people, searching for every reason not to believe in our fellow man or woman? This could be it, for we do not even fully believe in ourselves, so how could the next person be qualified to teach us something? Why are you in fear of finding the wonder that lies inside of you? Ask your Self this as well. Ask your Self why anyone would want to continue the cycle of life that has occupied this planet time after time. Why continue with the selfishness, the greed, the hate, the pain? Why the fear, the stress, the confusion? Why? Is it your knack for going against the grain that is preventing you from advancing spiritually, mentally and so on? Sometimes the "grain" is correct. I know some of you understand and know the truth, but you reject it out of fear. Maybe the cycle continues for money and status or comfort and safety. Is your job or career preventing you from making the proper change? I am fully aware that this writing will bother some due to the nature of their "business". The belief in "things" as a way of defining you at this point is silly and juvenile.

You cannot come up with a good reason to continue on the path we have been on. You cannot convince me that there is proper reason to be stuck in negativity. Yes, I am aware of the struggle and "forces" that influence us. I am aware of the difficulty in change. Yes I am aware of what the church says, and what your mother thinks, and what your "leader" has told you. I am aware of society's plans for you. However, I am also aware of the power you possess. And I believe that your power will overcome any obstacle, challenge, or "force" that is put in front of you. You are designed to win but have been conditioned to lose. I choose to believe in us and our design rather than the unnatural "force", which concededly is only powered and strengthened by our weak thoughts. Negativity and "evil" can only last but so long before nature destroys even that from within. For even "evil" will have its end on this Earth, so why not start to bring it to its knees now? You are assuming evil is only murder or a systematic conspiracy. No, evil is you being afraid of evil. Evil cannot defeat the righteous, not now and not ever. You believing in it and/or fearing it as strongly as you may, does not allow you to fully focus on the good. This lack of focus will one day create an error in you, if it has not done so already. Your Source should be reason enough to remove fear from your being, for your Source is alive in you. Stop contradicting the truth. Stop missing the mark that some of us are able to see so clearly. We are waiting for you to wake up. Some of you will quote religious texts word for word, but manage to still possess a lack. Why is this so? If you have the faith of a mustard seed, then why would you allow evil to find a way into your minds and hearts? Why, when you have been told to not be afraid? What are you putting your faith in? You will say "I am not afraid". Ok, but if you continuously discuss something or think of it, it is present in you. So why continuously discuss what is wrong and evil to the beat of obsession? You continuously give it power so therefore it is present thanks to you.

We have always had a choice, even if you have been too wrapped up to see it clearly. From the smallest decision to the largest one, a choice is always present.

Believe you are more than just flesh because of your Source. Believe in this power you possess. Believe you are supposed to be happy and in tune, but understand why you are not and fix your lack. Believe in your Self, you, the one true Self you possess. Find it; find this Self that is underneath the cloud the world has placed over you and others like you until now. Find your future. Find a future full of the right choices, and realize the way we and so many others have attempted to show you. I can see it, as can others, but can you? You have all you need to do so and you have all you need to create anew. We want you, but we only want you if you are willing to go and properly recondition your Self. We only want you if you are going to better your Self and better the future of others here on Earth. I do not mean to sound egotistical when informing you of our wants, but they are true. For whomever you believe in, if there indeed is someone or something you believe in, it or they probably want you with them at some point in time. If you are going to be present with us on this plane, we want you to be proper. This can help you now, and this can help you find your future. I want you to continue on your journey to find the truth, for there is more out there waiting for you. I want you to create a world of wonder, a world that has been missing for some time now. Imagine and dream, then do and live. Be well now and remember to travel fearlessly into your future. We will be watching, ever so patient and ever so understanding, waiting to welcome you when you get here.

A special Thanks to those who have assisted me in creating this work.

Editor - Katelyn Williams

Rear Cover Art - Jessica Lopez

Front Cover Art by William Autore

Made in the USA
Columbia, SC
15 November 2017